T38092

RIDGE AVENUE,
LONDON, N21 2RH
Tel: 360 8662

		16. OCT. 1980	
27. MAR 1981	-5. DEC. 1981		26. JAN. 1984
27. MAY 1981	-8. FEB. 1982	-6. DEC. 1982	
-6. JUN. 1981	15. MAR. 1982		-1. MAY 1984
		-5. MAY 1983	14. JUN. 1984
23. JUL. 1981 18. AUG. 1981	22. MAY 1982		4 14.8.84
	19. JUN. 1982	24. MAY 1983	17. SEP 1984
18. SEP 1981	19. JUL. 1982	-5. SEP 1983	
-1. OCT. 1981	14. AUG 1982		21. MAR. 1985
17. OCT. 1981	11. SEP. 1982	12. SEP. 1983	

LONDON BOROUGH OF ENFIELD
LIBRARY SERVICES

This book to be RETURNED on or before the latest date stamped unless a renewal has been obtained by personal call, post ~~or telepho~~ne, quoting the above number and the date due for return.

Collecting Football Programmes

Collecting Football Programmes

Phil Shaw

GRANADA
London Toronto Sydney New York

Granada Publishing Limited
Frogmore, St Albans, Herts AL2 2NF
and
3 Upper James Street, London W1R 4BP
866 United Nations Plaza, New York, NY 10017, USA
117 York Street, Sydney, NSW 2000, Australia
100 Skyway Avenue, Toronto, Ontario, Canada M9W 3A6
PO Box 84165, Greenside, 2034 Johannesburg, South Africa
61 Beach Road, Auckland, New Zealand

Published by Granada in 1980
Hardback ISBN 0 246 11399 5
Paperback ISBN 0 583 30424 9

Edited and designed by Boondoggle Limited
Copyright © Boondoggle Limited 1980

Set in Great Britain by the Yale Press Limited, London in
Linotron 202 Times Roman

Printed and bound in Hong Kong by
Wing King Tong Company Limited

All rights reserved. No part of this publication may be
reproduced, stored in a retrieval system, or transmitted, in any form
or by any means, electronic, mechanical, photocopying, recording
or otherwise, without the prior permission of the publishers.

Granada®
Granada Publishing®

London Borough
of Enfield
Public Libraries

T38092

**For Dave, Vanda
and Layla**

Contents

1: THE PROGRAMME REVOLUTION   8
Team-sheets in the 19th century; commercial awakening in the mid-1960s; Coventry's pioneering 'Sky Blue'; the spread of match-day magazines; Leeds catch up; newspaper-programmes; standardisation.

2: WHY COLLECT?   14
The programme's appeal as club's official organ; nostalgia; building a library of statistical information, pen pictures and photos; following progress of young players; learning how traditions are built; tracing changes in soccer and society.

3: CARING FOR YOUR COLLECTION   24
The 'dos' and 'don'ts, of storing programmes; how to avoid tearing, folding; how to record team changes; the big enemies – dirt, damp and sunlight; special care for very old issues; binding programmes; the problem of vouchers; sending programmes by post.

4: HOW TO COLLECT   30
Subscriptions; club shops; writing to the club; programme clubs – the advantages and drawbacks; replying to adverts; fairs, conventions and shops; 'pirates'.

5: SPECIALISING   36
All the homes and aways of one club for a season; one from each of the 92 League clubs; ex-League clubs; new members of the League; non-League; cup competitions; British clubs in Europe; international, foreign, prewar, 'derby' and testimonial issues.

6: THE INSIDE STORY   46
A behind-the-scenes look at how two programme editors – Gordon Ross (Arsenal) and Tony Thwaites (Halifax Town) – compile their clubs' issues.

7: EVERY PROGRAMME TELLS A STORY   55
Manchester United and the aftermath of Munich; Chelsea's red card experiment; madness at Old Trafford; Inverness Thistle in the national spotlight; Manchester United's programme sales records; the American approach; the end of Bradford Park Avenue; Gateshead and Accrington meet again; Leeds' notorious 12 changes; the 1923 FA Cup final; League new boys; the Centenarians; the top non-League issues; 'Programme of the Year' award winners.

8: DIRECTORY OF FOOTBALL LEAGUE PROGRAMMES   81
An A-Z guide; where to write for subscriptions or individual issues; club shops – where they are and when they're open; plus the addresses of the Scottish clubs with recommended programme clubs and shops.

1: The Programme Revolution

There was a time when your match-day reading would have taken just a couple of minutes to flick through. From the earliest editions published in the late 19th century programmes were, with a few honorable exceptions, dull, advert-packed, often no more than team-sheeets.

A small number of clubs, notably Aston Villa with their 'News & Record' – which even in 1906 was an informative 18-page edition – took great pride in presenting a stylish production with plenty of reading matter and statistics. West Ham, Arsenal, Millwall and Manchester United also published interesting pro grammes before the last war.

But on the whole programmes had progressed little by the 1960s. Only a tiny number of clubs featured action photographs, and most seemed to feel that as long as they managed to squeeze the day's teams, brief pen-pictures of the visitors and the fixture list in among the advertisements, then they had done their job.

The turning point came in 1966 with the staging of the World Cup in England. Before then only Arsenal and Chelsea, and to a lesser extent, Spurs, West Ham and Manchester United, appeared to realise the value of the club programme as a vehicle for communicating with the fans, making them feel an affinity to their club, or simply as a potential money-spinner.

The commercial explosion which accompanied the World Cup in England made many people in the game sit up and realise that there was an enormous market for well-designed, attractive merchandise. That year millions of key-rings, mugs, ashtrays and books portraying the tournament's mascot, a lion called 'World Cup Willie', were sold to a public that was beginning to rediscover its passion for Britian's national game.

The lesson was not lost on Jimmy Hill, then manager of Coventry City. As well as lifting City from the Third Division to the First in just four seasons, Hill set about the commercial reorganisation of the club. A club shop, express trains to away matches complete with bingo sessions and a disco, 'live' pre-match

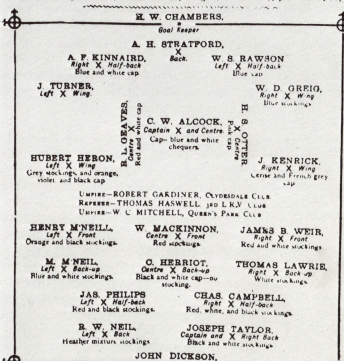

Above: *Possibly the oldest existing programme – for a friendly between Queen's Park and Wanderers on 9 October 1875. As players did not wear numbers, they were identified by the colour of their socks or the kind of cap they wore. It wasn't until February 1876 – nearly nine years after their formation – that Queen's Park finally lost a match.*

entertainment by local pop groups – Hill didn't miss a trick.

Coventry's pride and joy, however, was the 'Sky Blue', the first of what we know today as match-day magazines. It appeared first for Coventry's opening home First Division game in 1967, against Sheffield United, and was regarded as a 'bit pricey' at one shilling (5p). It was larger than its predecessors – a mini-magazine in fact.

The 'Sky Blue' had excellent photographic content, which included pictures of the visitors and double-page spreads of action from their previous fixture. There was an up-to-date article on Coventry's opponents for the day, as well as pen-pictures, news from other first Division clubs, a wealth of statistical detail, a 'where are they now?' feature on City players of the past, road maps for travelling fans, and even a women's section.

Unfortunately Hill resigned to take up a top position in the sports division of London Weekend Television on the eve of the publication of the very first 'Sky Blue'. Without him, Coventry were to struggle on the field in their first season of top-class football, but their programme soon became the envy of several more 'established' clubs.

The format was quickly adopted by West Bromwich Albion ('Albion News'), Wolves ('Molinews'), Sheffield Wednesday ('Wednesday World') and Sunderland ('Roker Review').

Strangely enough Leeds, Liverpool and Manchester United – the top sides in the country at the end of the 1960s – were either oblivious to the 'Sky Blue revolution' or chose to ignore it, and continued to produce relatively old-fashioned programmes.

The Leeds programme was arguably the least interesing in all four divisions. Its contents had scarcely changed since the time when United were scratching around in the lower reaches of the Second Division 10 years earlier.

Then in 1973 Peter Fay, one-time Football League press officer and an experienced journalist, was appointed public relations officer at Elland Road, and immediately set about changing Leeds' conservative image.

'Without wishing to denigrate the work of those local journalists who had produced the programme until then – for the princely sum of £12.50 per issue – it really was dreadful,' says Fay. 'It had about as much appeal as a local authority pamphlet on sewage cleaning and distribution.'

Programme collectors had given their verdict on Leeds' archaic

The changing face of the Coventry City programme. **Top left:** An edition from 1955-56. Over half its 12 pages were taken up by adverts. **Above:** A City programme from 1960-61, which had a similarly high proportion of advertising. **Left:** Jimmy Hill has come and gone, and the 'Sky Blues' have moved from Division 3 to Division 1. The 'Sky Blue' matchday magazine for 1967-68 had 24 pages, packed with articles, photographs and statistics – a real step forward for programmes.

publication. The members of the British Programme Club voted it one of the worst in the League in a poll. Fay determined to change that situation.

'I introduced an entirely new style of publication, just as Coventry had done before us. It was not only designed to be attractive, but a good read too. So we had a largish edition with a full colour cover, selling at 10p. That was double the price of its predecessor, but we had no adverse reaction at all.

'The magazine was carefully planned. I introduced in-depth articles by the visiting managers, and Don Revie had a regular column which was fairly hard hitting. So not only did you get Don's point of view, but, say, Bill Shankly's too. Too many clubs use the manager's column as an excuse to fill up some space. You still read things like "How nice it is to welcome our visitors today", when you know the two managers can't stand the sight of each other.

'Leeds' magazine always had a lengthy feature on one of their own stars. I wasn't very interested to know what Billy Bremner's favourite foods were, or what John Giles liked listening to on his stereo, and I don't think the Leeds public were either. So the features were written informatively.

'Instead of selling to 50% of the Leeds crowd, we started to sell to 75%. During my three seasons with United, starting in 1973-74, the programme made a total profit of over £67,000, which was ploughed into facilities. And it went from one of the worst to best in the British Programme Club awards in the very first year, which is something to be proud of.'

Nowadays, the programme 'revolution' encompasses clubs from the lower divisions and even some from outside the Football League, although ironically the one that started the ball rolling, the 'Sky Blue', has slipped behind. Programmes have become such big business that several firms now specialise in programme production. One company may be engaged in producing programmes for as many as five or six clubs, and indeed one Blackburn firm, Sportscene, produced newspaper-style programmes for clubs as far away as Walsall and Northampton in 1979-80. The newspaper format has never been very popular with collectors, because of its size and the fact that they have to be folded. A more common complaint about the modern programme, however, is that the degree of standardisation which results from one firm designing and printing for several clubs has robbed the programme of some of its individuality.

Top: *Derby County's 'Ram', a newspaper-style programme which is also sold in newsagents prior to a match.* **Centre:** *Doncaster Rovers' newspaper-programme, one of six similar efforts produced by a Blackburn firm in the 1979-80 season.* **Left:** *Leeds United's matchday magazine for 1979-80, with a different colour photograph on each cover.*

2: Why Collect?

For thousands of football fans, arriving at a match and finding that all the programmes have been sold is almost as disappointing as seeing their team lose. Some will cheerfully miss kick-off if joining a long queue ensures that they get their programme. And it is not uncommon, even in the age of the 30p match-day magazine, to spot visiting supporters spending pounds on buying up copies for their friends back home.

After the game, win or lose, whether at Liverpool or Hartlepool, Rangers or Raith Rovers, very few of those programme purchasers will throw their copies away. Since the war, and particularly over the last 15 years, collecting soccer programmes has developed into a major hobby, with thousands of pounds changing hands each year and 'programmaniacs' aged from seven to seventy joining in the fun.

So what is the attraction? After all, the main function of the programme is to inform the spectator of the terms for the match in question, so that once the game is over the programme is of little practical use to anyone – right?

Wrong. While the official programme or match-day magazine is indeed a record, or a souvenir, of a particular fixture, it is also much more than that. Badges, rosettes, scarves, records and many other items that are available to football fans are very often commercially produced by organisations who have little or no connection with the club. But the programme has traditionally been the voice of the club, their official publication. As such it has become the average supporter's strongest link with the club he or she follows week in and week out.

Most experienced collectors take programmes very seriously. But is shouldn't be forgotten that they can provide pleasure too, and that is as good a reason as any to start saving. Just flicking through an old issue can stir up a whole string of memories and settle numerous arguments. Imagine, for example, looking back in ten years time at the programme for 1979 League Cup tie at Highbury between Arsenal and Leeds United, when the Gunners won 7-0. Who was in goal for Leeds that fateful night? A quick glance at the team line-ups

Above: *The first-ever copy of the 'Villa News & Record', published by Aston Villa for the League match with Blackburn on 1 September 1906. Priced at one penny ('old' money), it contained a full-page photo of Villa skipper Howard Spencer; a report on a cricket match between Villa and Aston Unity, which Villa won thanks to an unbeaten century by J. B. Higgins; a breakdown of gate receipts and wage bills of all the top clubs; and, intriguingly, fixture lists for Villa's neighbours and rivals – Birmingham, Wolves and WBA.*

reveals that the unfortunate keeper was David Harvey. How had Arsenal been playing before they tore Leeds apart? The results list shows that they had failed to score in their previous two home matches.

Another reason for collecting programmes is that it is possible to build up a fascinating historical picture, both of the club you support and of the game in general. Most club programmes now carry detailed statistical information – line-ups, substitutes, scorers, attendances and appearances – as well as photographs of recent games and news about the reserves and youth team. If you want to find out which player scored in a particular fixture, the programme usually offers an easy-to-check instant reference work.

It's fun, too, to look back on how famous names fared long before they ever broke into the big-time, which you can do by checking previous seasons' reserve and junior appearance lists.

More and more clubs now run features about their past. In 1978-79, for example, Manchester United ran a series called 'The great ones down the years with the Reds' which provided a season-by-season breakdown of every game the club had played in its 100-year history, complete with lists of appearances and League tables. You often hear supporters talk about their club's 'tradition'; by collecting programmes and reading about the great names and games from yesteryear you build up a picture of exactly how that 'tradition' was built.

If you can obtain issues from the 1950s and 1960s you may also be able to trace something of the changes in the sport over the years. In the early postwar years, programme covers often featured sketches of players attired in shirts with rugby-style collars and buttons, long baggy shorts, and big heavy boots which looked more appropriate for fell-walking or mining than for scoring goals. As the 1960s approached, the drawing would be replaced by a black and white photo and the kit had also been up-dated and streamlined. Lighter, V-neck shirts with short sleeves, less cumbersome shorts and lightweight boots were now the order of the day. They eventually gave way to round-neck shirts with long sleeves, which in turn have been replaced by the flashy outfits now sported by many clubs. Today, of course, it's not a drawing but very often a full-colour photo on the cover.

The same applies to the changes which have so dramatically changed the face of so many grounds since the 1950s. Many clubs

Left column: *Note the changes in attire for both fan and player in the cover illustration of Manchester United's 'United Review' over the years.*
Right column: *Programmes from Rotherham (1956-57), Doncaster (1961-62) and Plymouth (1968-69) reflect the evolution of modern strips.*

Above: *Huddersfield Town reached the First Division in 1970, holding their own against the likes of Manchester United, Leeds and Arsenal before slipping back into the Second Division at the end of 1971-72.*

Above: *Northampton in the First Division, 1965-66.* **Right:** *Ipswich in the Third Division (South). 1955-56.*

Above: *Huddersfield's decline continued. Less than two years after playing host to Manchester United, Town were battling for Third Division points against Port Vale. Two years later they slipped into Division 4.*

Above: *Luton v Darlington and Brighton v Bradford Park Avenue – Fourth Division programmes from 1967-68 and 1963-64 respectively, showing how dramatically fortunes can change in football.*

have featured photos of terracing which have been replaced in many cases by smart new stands with tip-up seats. By seeking out old programmes you can get an idea of what things were like long before you were born.

Programmes can also be extremely revealing in showing how the game itself has evolved. Right up to the mid 1960s most people still tended to think in terms of teams playing two full-backs, three half-backs and five forwards, including two wingers. The number five was always centre-half, and number nine was expected to lead the attack and score goals aplenty. Yet by the time England won the World Cup in 1966, it was clear that managers were opting for tactical formations like 4-3-3 or 4-4-2, in which the player wearing number 11 might play in a defensive midfield role rather than on the left wing. Sure enough, clubs gradually began to simply list the teams vertically in the programme without attempting to assign the 'old' positions to them.

Older programmes are also a fascinating guide to changes in society. Pick up a Bolton Wanderers programme from 1956 and look at the adverts for British Railways' excursions to away matches. Bolton to London cost 30 shillings (£1.50) return, whereas today on British Rail it would cost nearer £10. 'Tea 3d, (1½p), Coffee 4d (2p), Ham Sandwich 6d (2½p)' boasted another Bolton programme cover from the 1950s. Millwall's carried advertising for a money lender – *'I lend money – £5 and upwards'* was his blunt slogan – and for the *'British Home for Incurables',* a charity exclusively for 'the middle classes'.

The Stanley Matthews-endorsed football boots advertised in Mansfield's programme in 1963 would set you back 65/6d (£3.27½), whereas nowadays a pair endorsed by Kevin Keegan or Mario Kempes could cost you well over £20. And Manchester United's cover illustration in the 1950s and 1960s portrayed a player shaking hands with a supporter; it is interesting to see how the artist had to change his sketch as fashions changed.

On a more sombre note, the Northern Ireland v Spain match in 1971 was played at Hull (they later played internationals at Everton and Fulham too) because of the situation in Ulster, and the programme cover is a record of this.

Another example of how programmes can reflect society is illustrated on the cover of what looks like just another Millwall issue from January 1974. A closer examination reveals that the

Above: *The Sheffield Wednesday programme for 1964-65 depicted a view of Hillsborough's impressive new cantilever stand. Within ten seasons the Owls had slipped into Division 3 – to be joined later by Sheffield United.*

game (against Fulham) was played on a Sunday morning – the first League match ever played on that day. The reason? The government had placed restrictions on the use of electricity as a result of the miners' strike, and several clubs took the opportunity to experiment with Sunday soccer. Inside the programme there are references to the 'three-day working week' and the 'current rail crisis' too, further evidence of troubled times.

Apart from becoming more expert on the team you support, collecting programmes also helps you to build up a library of information about other clubs. 'Pen pictures' of the visiting side are featured by almost every home club, often accompanied by a team picture. If you can collect a complete set of your team's programmes for a season, you may also have the biographies of the first-team players of all the other clubs at your disposal.

It's often exciting, too, to obtain issues from 'big' games, such as cup finals, internationals or foreign fixtures. More than watching on TV or reading the newspaper reports, having an official programme gives a real sense of 'being there' – a permanent memento of an historic occasion. Just as interesting to many collectors are the programmes issued by small clubs playing amateur or semi-professional football before just a few hundred spectators, with even fewer programmes printed.

Programme collecting need not be an expensive hobby, although inflation has obviously taken its toll, with higher postal charges and an increase in printing costs which has seen prices rocket in the last five years. But it's important to remember that every programme you save has a value to somebody, and should be looked upon as an investment for the future. If you ever decide to sell, you can be sure there will be no shortage of buyers.

Above: *It's unlikely, though not impossible, that Bury and Leeds United will meet again in League football as they did in Division 2 in 1952-53.*

3: Caring For Your Collection

As your programme collection begins to grow in size and the older issues start to gather value, it becomes increasingly important to keep them in good condition.

It is no use cramming today's match-day magazines into an old shoe-box where the corners may become bent or torn, or leaving them lying around to gather dust or in a spot where they may become stained by drinks or food. Apart from anything else, if the time ever comes when you decide to sell your collection, damaged copies will seriously hinder your chances of getting a good price for them. Nor will any serious collector be keen to accept a 'soiled' programme in exchange for an issue that you may really want.

So it is vital to look after your programmes. Many fans like to fill in the team changes when they attend a match, and some record the attendance and other details afterwards. Unfortunately, writing on a programme in any way always diminishes its value considerably.

If possible, take any alterations and details of the result, scorers or attendance down on a separate sheet of paper. Slip it inside the programme, or attach it with a paper clip. Avoid using staples, as this can lead to tearing if you try to remove the paper later on.

If you really must record changes on your programme, use a pencil. Even then, try not to mark the cover at all.

Similarly, you should resist the temptation to identify the programme as belonging to you by printing your name on the front, or by numbering them. As you acquire more and more programmes and the numbers become higher, such markings take up a lot of room and look ugly. Remember, too, that they are totally meaningless to other collectors, and could spoil your chances of obtaining the swaps you require.

Always remember not to fold or crease programmes if you can possibly avoid doing so, It's very tempting, especially if you are standing in a packed crowd, to roll up your programme or to fold it over and slip it in your pocket. Do try to take a carrier bag and/or a large envelope in which to keep your copy. This way you'll be able

In direct contrast with the large magazine-style programmes of today, many clubs favoured a pocket-sized edition during the 1960s.
Above: *Notts County, 1961-62; Sunderland, 1964-65; Crystal Palace, 1961-62; Reading, 1963-64; Portsmouth, 1964-65; Rochdale, 1964-65; Barnsley, 1962-63; Northampton Town, 1964-65; Swindon Town, 1964-65; Ipswich Town, 1963-64. Usually these mini-programmes measured 140 mm × 110 mm.*

to keep it dry if it rains, and you won't get grease, sweat or dirty thumb prints all over your programme. And if, as occasionally happens, you should drop it, it won't get covered in mud.

At home, it is vital to store your collection in a sensible place. The big enemies are dirt, damp and sunlight.

Try to keep your programmes in a place out of reach of younger brothers and sisters who are too young to understand your hobby, and may decide to do a nice drawing for mum all over the cover of your most treasured item.

Put your collection in a dry spot. You mustn't leave your programmes on a window-sill where they may become damp from dripping condensation. If they are left in such a place, rust from the staples soon creates brown stains. And if a programme gets even slightly wet, once it dries the paper may become brittle or crinkly.

It is equally important not to leave any of your collection lying where strong sunlight may get at it. Heat – whether from the sun or from central heating – tends to make the paper curl up in much the same way that a record warps when similarly exposed. You will also find that colours fade badly in the sun, and you could end up with pink Liverpool programmes.

The sensible method of storing programmes is to keep them flat and unfolded, perhaps in a large cardboard box (your local supermarket will usually let you take one, but ask first), or in a drawer or on a shelf. If a friend offers you a creased copy, don't turn your nose up at it; if you keep it pressed underneath others in a pile, the folds will smoothe out to a certain extent.

If you are fortunate enough to be given some old programmes it is particularly important to follow these guidelines, since the paper on which they are printed is often of poor quality. If you can obtain a suitable polythene bag, it is worth keeping *individual* copies of old programmes inside to prevent any further deterioration in their condition.

Some collectors who specialise in trying to obtain complete sets of one particular club's games favour the use of binders. In fact, some clubs, such as Fulham in the mid-1960s, had the foresight to produce attractive 'box binders' with the team's name printed on the spine. But were such containers are unavailable, collectors are sometimes tempted to secure their set for the season in book form.

If you want to bind yours, do not use glue or a hole-puncher.

Top left: *Rodney Marsh and George Best on the cover of Fulham's programme, 1976-77.*
Top right: *Chelsea salute Stanley Matthews in the Stoke winger's final season, 1964-65.*
Above: *Chelsea pay tribute to Bobby Charlton on the occasion of his last appearance for Manchester United, 1972-73;*
Left: *Best again – from his home debut for Hibs, 1979-80.*

For a start, both methods mean that the programmes are irrevocably defaced. Also, if the time comes when you feel you want to part with those programmes, you'll find that you will get a much better price by selling them individually rather than in a bound volume.

So think twice before binding your programmes, and use a loose-leaf folder from which copies can be removed easily and without damage.

The introduction by many clubs of a voucher system has created new problems for programme collectors. Most of the top clubs now use vouchers for supporters to cut out, collect and use to be eligible for tickets for important matches.

However neatly the programme is clipped, the removal of a token considerably reduces its value and spoils its appearance. The only certain way of avoiding this kind of damage is to buy two programmes – and that can prove expensive. However many you buy, don't cut vouchers until a big game comes up and you know for certain that you are going to have to use that method to get a ticket. Make sure you cut carefully and don't tear the paper in any way.

If you are swapping programmes by post, it is essential to pack them properly. Don't try to force them into an evelope too small to hold them. The programmes will almost certainly be damaged, and they may even become lost in the post because the envelope has split open. You'll find that it pays to observe this rule, for other collectors will be reluctant to exchange programmes by mail with you if they have been stung once.

So remember the golden rules of caring for your collection: don't write on them, store them sensibly, keeping them away from damp and heat, and try to avoid handling them too much. If you want to bind them, use a method that enables you to take out individual copies. Always pack programmes for posting so that they will arrive in the sort of condition in which *you* would like to receive them.

If you don't look after your collection, they won't be worth nearly as much when you want to swap or sell. You may not be able to picture the day coming when you don't want to carry on collecting programmes, but it does happen. Follow the guidelines, and you'll not only get the right price but the programmes will also give another collector great pleasure.

Top left: *Millwall, 1958-59.* **Top right:** *Wolves, 1965-66.* **Above left:** *Notts County, 1974-75.* **Above right:** *Barnsley, 1970-71.* **Centre:** *Hull City, 1956-57.*

4: How To Collect

Whether you've made up your mind to specialise in one particular area or decided just to collect whatever takes your fancy, the task confronting you is how to lay your hands on the programmes you want. Some issues, particularly pre-1960 copies or those published by now-defunct clubs, may prove impossible to obtain. Yet there are several 'dos' and 'don'ts' of which you should be aware when building a programme collection.

If you want to concentrate on the home programmes of one club, check the directory at the back of this book to see whether they run an annual subscription service whereby they will send you a copy after each match in return for a lump sum at the start of the season. Most First and Second Division clubs operate subscriptions, with several from the lower divisions following suit.

A subscription could cost you £6 or over, but at least then your programme will be sent automatically through the post each week without your having to lift a finger.

If you also want to get that club's aways in order to build a complete set for the season, the job becomes slightly more difficult. If you are able to go to your team's home matches, visit the club shop; most clubs sell programmes in their shops, several of which are also open during the week (see directory for details). Many clubs co-operate with each other by swapping programmes. For example, when Newport County visit Halifax Town, they normally take a batch of 100-300 programmes to sell back at Newport to fans who were unable to make the journey, and vice-versa. This system appears to be more widespread and better organised among the 'smaller' clubs.

If this method is not practical for you, you should try writing to the club which your team is visiting. There are several important guidelines to follow to ensure success. First, do not write weeks or months after the game. If you do, the chances are that the one you want will be sold out, or that the away club will have taken any unsold programmes to sell at their club shop. Always remember to write two or three days before the game.

Your letter should be clearly written or printed, brief, polite and to the point. For example:

> 8, Smithson Street,
> Churchtown,
> Fairshire.
>
> Dear Sir or Madam,
> Please could you send me a programme of this week's Everton v Arsenal match. I enclose a postal order for 25p plus a SAE. Many thanks,
> Yours sincerely,
> Brian Collector.

Resist the temptation to write anything about the game or the club. Your letter will be handled by a busy office worker who is probably dealing with several similar requests as well as the club's other administrative business. They simply don't have time to answer queries about players or past games.

It is absolutely essential to send a postal order (or cheque) and an SAE (stamped, self-addressed envelope). It ought to go without saying that you should pay for your programmes, but many clubs do get 'cheeky' requests – not only asking for free programmes, but also for badges and photos. If you don't send a money order or the equivalent in stamps, you'll almost certainly be disappointed. Avoid sending coins by post: postal orders are more expensive, but coins can cause the envelope to tear so that your money falls out.

Most clubs prefer you to send an SAE. This should be no smaller than 254mm x 177mm, with your own address printed clearly on it and with adequate postage. However, with the increase in programme size, you may find that the programme has been folded in order to fit it into the envelope, so if you can get a supply of 306mm x 229mm envelopes, so much the better. A few clubs will accept orders for individual copies for which they provide the envelope, but unless you know this to be the case, enclose a SAE.

If, at the end of the season, you have missed out on a couple of away programmes due to a sell-out on the day, try writing to the appropriate supporters club. A polite letter explaining that you are a collector who needs help in completing a set and asking whether one of their members would be prepared to part with his or her copy often brings results. Address your letter to the Supporters Club, c/o the football club in question, and you may strike lucky.

Failing that, the best method of tracking down the programmes you want is probably to join a programme club. The established, reliable clubs offer a wide range of old and new programmes from all over the world which you can purchase at reasonable prices, and a means of getting in touch with other 'programmaniacs' to arrange suitable swaps.

The biggest and best of these clubs is the British Programme Club. Based in Hull, the BPC has been in operation since 1961 and now has premises near Hull City's ground, with thousands of programmes in stock. The BPC is divided into two sections: one for 'serious' collectors (called 'full members') who are prepared to spend considerable time and money on collecting, the other for virtual 'beginners' ('associate members') who get the chance to build their collections by buying programmes from the club at discount prices. Non-members are also eligible to buy programmes from the BPC, usually at ground prices.

Programme clubs often buy up complete collections, some going back many years. They also purchase considerable quantities of surplus programmes from football clubs. Some programme clubs will send out lists of old programmes for which you can bid, as at an auction. If you become serious enough about collecting this method is highly recommended, but if you're just starting it's probably better to concentrate on buying fairly recent items from the regular lists they send out.

The clubs listed in this book are all completely trustworthy and have a good record of helping young collectors. However, be warned: from time to time, you'll see ads for programme clubs in soccer magazines. Some of these are either badly and irresponsibly run, and a few are downright swindles. So always write for details before sending any money.

Another way to build your collection is to reply to adverts from programme dealers. Resist taking short cuts in your collecting by taking up offers of 'incredible bargains' which seem to offer something for next to nothing. These offers rarely live up to their promise: if they did, there would be precious little financial reward in it for the dealer concerned.

Keep an eye out for details of programme 'fairs' or 'conventions' to be held in your area. These are held at fairly regular intervals,

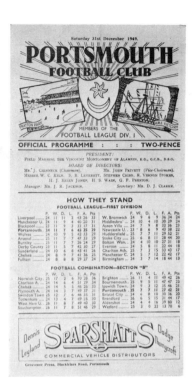

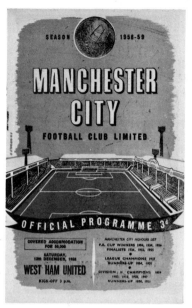

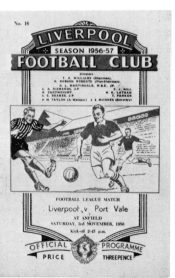

Above left: *A Portsmouth programme from 1949-50, when the club went on to win the Football League championship. At the time of this match against Middlesbrough, Pompey stood fourth, two points behind Blackpool and Manchester United, and four adrift of Liverpool.*
Above: *Manchester City, 1958-59.*
Left: *Liverpool v Port Vale, a Second Division match from 1956-57. At the time Liverpool stood 13th in the table, with Vale 19th. Above the Reds at the time were Nottingham Forest (2nd behind Leicester), Bristol Rovers (4th), Doncaster Rovers (7th) and Lincoln City, who were in 10th spot.*

often at non-League clubs or in supporters clubs' premises. At a good one, several dealers will have stalls selling their speciality. Some actually run programme shops on a full-time basis, and a selection of the major shops appears elsewhere in this book. If you're planning to visit a shop, make a list of the programmes – or clubs – you're interested in, because if you go in and just buy at random, you could run up quite a bill. Many a young collector has been dazzled into over-spending by a colourful array of programmes.

Be on your guard for two things when buying programmes – 'pirate' editions and forgeries. 'Pirate' programmes are produced with the sole intention of conning the public. They are nothing to do with the clubs involved in the match, and are usually sold at big cup matches. Visiting supporters, unaware of the host club's selling arrangements, see a man shouting 'programme!' and have no reason to suspect that he is anything but an official seller. Having parted with their cash, they open the programme to find a shoddy production containing little interesting reader matter. The usual format is pen-pictures of star players, most of whom have no connection with the fixture whatsoever and irrelevant lists of League champions. These programmes are absolutely worthless, so watch out for the tell-tale signs like the pirates' use of the word 'souvenir' instead of 'official'.

Forgeries and reproductions are turning up more and more as the hobby grows in popularity. Reproductions are frequently labelled as such, but unfortunately, 'fakes' aren't so easy to spot. However, if you are offered a pre-1950 programme in shiny, mint condition, then the chances are it is a reprint. Like 'pirate' programmes, they have no value as collector's items although they make fascinating reading material.

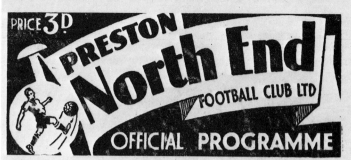

Above: *The Preston North End edition for the FA Cup 4th round tie against Bradford City in the 1958-59 season. Tom Finney, depicted here in cartoon form, won 76 England caps while a Preston player and is now club president.*

5: Specialising

In an ideal world, it would be possible to obtain a copy of every programme ever printed. Unfortunately, the cost of doing so would be massive, to say nothing of the storage problems. So whilst you should never refuse if a friend offers you a programme free, it is wise to remember that you just can't collect everything. The purpose of this section is to suggest some interesting areas in which you may choose to specialise.

If you support one particular Football League team, you may like to try to obtain a complete set of their home programmes for one season – the 21 League issues (23 if you follow a Third or Fourth Division club), plus cup games, friendlies and testimonials. If you live locally and attend the matches, you can get your copy at the ground. If you can't go, then ask somebody who is going to purchase an extra copy, making sure to give him the correct money beforehand. If you live some distance away, you will have to write to your chosen club in advance, although several now offer a subscription service.

It's always fascinating to see how other clubs see your team, so why not try to obtain a copy of the programme for every away game they play? Then you will have an entire season in programmes, and you will have built another set – one issue from each club in the division. Club shops are a good source of 'aways' since many clubs bring back a supply from each away trip. Many collectors prefer to make sure by writing to the home club. Better still, if you have a friend who is travelling to the game, ask him to bring one back for you.

One of the most popular aspects of collecting is to obtain at least one copy produced by each of the 92 Football League clubs. Some ambitious collectors develop this idea and try to get a programme for each club, each season. However, it is as well not to take on too much too soon.

You may notice in older issues the names of several clubs who no longer appear in the League tables, and pursuing their programmes is one of the most fascinating ways in which you can

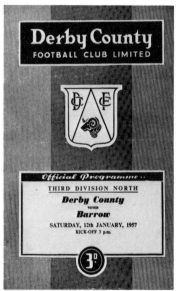
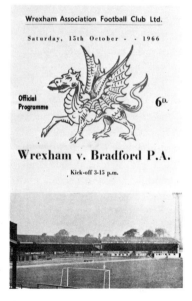

Above: *Carlisle v Gateshead, 1956-57; Gillingham v Accrington, 1961-62; Derby v Barrow, 1956-57; Wrexham v Bradford Park Avenue, 1966-67. The away club in each case were later to lose their Football League place.*

specialise. Since the war, seven Northern clubs have lost their Football League places. They are New Brighton (who last appeared in the Third North in 1959-51), Gateshead (not re-elected to the Fourth after 1959-60), Accrington Stanley (original League members, who went bankrupt midway through 1961-62), Bradford Park Avenue (last season 1969-70), Barrow (1971-72), Workington (1976-77) and Southport (1977-78).

The last three play on – Workington and Southport in the Northern Premier League, Barrow in the Alliance – but Bradford's ground has stood empty, vandalised and overgrown with weeds since the club folded in 1974, the year that Gateshead also became defunct, although a new club of the same name competes in the NPL. A new Accrington Stanley club was formed in 1968, and play in the Cheshire League along with New Brighton.

The programmes of teams entering the League are of equal interest to many collectors, particularly their first match and issues from their non-League days. When the next new club is elected, you could try to collect a complete set of their first season's homes and aways. Keep an eye out too for Southern League programmes of Oxford United, Cambridge United, Hereford and Wimbledon, as well as those published by Peterborough United in their Midland League days and Wigan's from the time when they played in the Cheshire League and the NPL.

One way to beat the rush which inevitably occurs when a club fails to win re-election to the League is to purchase issues of clubs who are reported to be in heavy financial trouble, or who frequently have to apply for re-election. In 1972-73 for example, debt-stricken Newport County looked as though they might fold at one point, although thankfully they managed to survive. Clubs like Rochdale, Halifax Town and Crewe Alexandra have been under similar pressure in recent years, as well as having poor playing records.

Nobody wants to see these clubs die, but as a collector is makes sense to obtain copies of their programmes, and of some of those aspiring to replace them. In that respect, it is worth writing to the Alliance Premier League, which includes all the top non-League teams in the country, requesting the addresses and present prices of the programmes published by their member clubs.

If you decide to specialise in collecting non-League programmes, you must realise the size of your task. There are upwards of

Top left: *Gateshead v Chesterfield, 1956-57. Gateshead were not re-elected to the League at the end of 1959-60 despite the fact that Oldham and Hartlepool finished below them.* **Top right:** *Bradford Park Avenue v York City, 1956-57. That season Derby finished top of the Third Division (North), with Avenue 20th.* **Above left:** *Workington v Hull, 1957-58. The kick-off was 5.45 because Workington had no floodlights.* **Above right:** *Accrington v Bradford City, 1961-62. Within weeks the club had folded.*

300 semi-professional and amateur clubs publishing programmes in Britain, some on a regular basis, others only for FA Cup, FA Trophy or FA Vase matches. Many of these programmes are typewritten and produced on duplicating machines. Very few carry photos or pen-pictures, although several Alliance Premier League clubs publish editions worthy of the Football League status they seek.

Another interesting way in which to specialise is to focus on a particular competition. Set yourself a target – every FA Cup or Football League Cup programme for one season, from the first round proper through to the final. It is possible, though rather time-consuming and expensive – the kind of venture perhaps best left until you have sufficient time and money to follow it through.

Another word of warning: months of patient collecting, writing to obscure non-League outfits who have reached the first round, can be spoiled if you fail to secure just one programme. A lower division side at home to a top First Division club can often mean a programme sell-out, particularly if the visitors happen to be Manchester United or Liverpool.

Other areas you can choose to specialise in include 'big match' issues, foreign club programmes or those from matches featuring British teams against overseas visitors, and, if you're prepared to splash out on your hobby, prewar and wartime programmes. Some 'collectors' like to concentrate on cup finals, semi-finals and internationals. The problem with that option is that although hundreds of thousands of copies are printed for the FA Cup final, they quickly sell out, and copies from as recently as 1970 have become relatively scarce. The programme for that year's Leeds United v Chelsea replay at Old Trafford could cost you upwards of £3 from a dealer. Wembley programmes cost as much as 50p on match-days anyway, so take this into consideration before you become a 'big match' specialist.

The cost of collecting foreign editions can also be high, especially with postal charges and cover prices soaring all the time. It can also prove frustrating because in several European countries, notably Italy and Spain, football programmes as we know them are rarely produced. So there would be little point in writing to Inter-Milan, Juventus, Real Madrid or Barcelona, although most of the better known French, German and Dutch clubs do publish programmes. Remember, too, that even if you can obtain foreign

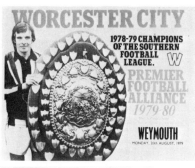

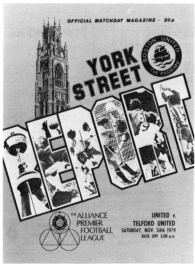

Above: *Alliance Premier League programmes from the inaugural season, 1979-80.*
Top left: *Worcester City v Weymouth.*
Top right: *Scarborough v Bath City.*
Above left: *Altrincham v Crewe Alexandra – an FA Cup tie.*
Above right: *Boston v Telford.*
Left: *Stafford v AP Leamington.*

issues, the fun of reading through will be somewhat lessened unless you are familiar with the language.

An easier method of obtaining information and photographs of foreign teams is to specialise in European Cup, Cup Winners Cup or UEFA Cup matches played in Britain. Several clubs do special editions for such ties, containing articles on soccer abroad. You could extend this theme in your collection by sending off for programmes of matches played between British sides and touring foreign clubs. For example, Ajax, the Dutch champions, played at West Bromwich Albion prior to the 1978-79 season, while American teams like Cosmos, Los Angeles Aztecs and Tulsa Roughnecks have all played in England. These 'one-offs' between clubs who don't normally meet are well worth looking out for.

A gift of some prewar or wartime programmes may encourage you to specialise in that direction. Although they are invariably printed on poor paper and are in grubby condition – as well as lacking most of the editorial features, statistics and photos we expect today – these old programmes have a marvellous historical 'feel' to them. Unfortunately it can be a costly line to pursue: £5 is probably the very least you could expect to pay for a Chelsea or Arsenal programme from the immediate prewar era.

Programmes from testimonials and local 'derbies' offer two interesting sidelines you may choose to pursue. Most of the top internationals and players who have completed ten years' service with one club are awarded a match in recognition. The attraction of such programmes is that they frequently contain archive photos and statistical breakdowns of the players concerned – so you will have the careers of the great players of your time to browse through.

Exactly what constitutes a 'derby' is debatable. Certainly all games between clubs from the same city qualify for the description, but so too must clashes between Newcastle United and Sunderland or Wolves and West Bromwich Albion. One possibility is to go for a set of London 'derbies': Arsenal and Wimbledon may never meet in League football, but they may well be paired together in a cup competition, while recent ups and downs have thrown together such unlikely league opponents as Spurs and Millwall. Specialising in 'derbies' can be particularly rewarding because clubs often produce special issues for meetings with their neighbours. For example, Sheffield United's edition for the game against Sheffield Wednesday in 1970-71 contained a reproduction of the programme from their 1911 'derby'.

Of course you don't have to specialise at all. One of the most pleasurable ways to collect is to look through the fixture lists a week in advance and pick out interesting matches. Look for unlikely games between big clubs on their way down and minnows enjoying a rare season in a higher grade. The 1970s threw up such unthinkable League pairings as Aston Villa v Rochdale, Palace v Halifax, Tottenham Hotspur v Mansfield, Hereford v Nottingham Forest, York City v Manchester United and Cambridge United v West Ham, as well as unusual 'derbies' that might never happen again like those between Oldham Athletic and Manchester United in 1974-75, or Walsall and Villa in 1970-71.

Whichever course you choose to follow, try not to take on anything outside your financial means, and remember that programme collecting is supposed to be fun too. With a little foresight and planning you should be able to come by the programmes you want in order to build an interesting and worthwhile collection.

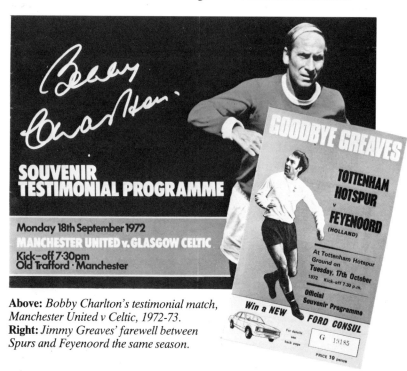

Above: *Bobby Charlton's testimonial match, Manchester United v Celtic, 1972-73.*
Right: *Jimmy Greaves' farewell between Spurs and Feyenoord the same season.*

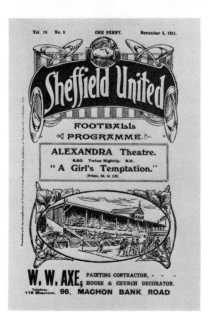

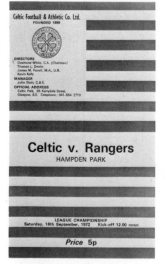
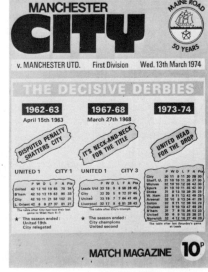

Top left: *Sheffield United v Sheffield Wednesday, 1911-12.* **Top right:** *Notts County v Nottingham Forest, 1973-74.* **Above left:** *Celtic v Rangers at Hampden, 1972-73.* **Above right:** *City v United, 1973-74.*

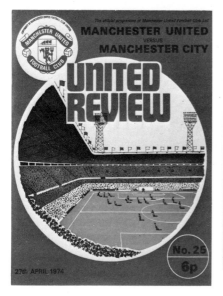

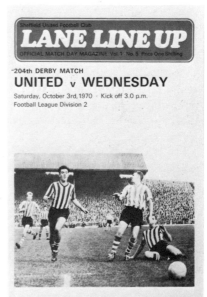

Top left: *Manchester United v Manchester City, 1973-74.* **Top right:** *Stoke City v Port Vale, 1954-55.* **Above left:** *Bradford City v Bradford Park Avenue, 1966-67.* **Above right:** *United v Wednesday, 1970-71.*

6: The Inside Story

For most people involved in football, Sunday is strictly a day of rest: a day when the tensions and emotions of Saturday afternoon, if not actually forgotten, are pushed into the back of the mind before the weekly grind begins again in earnest on Monday. While the rest of the football world enjoys a lie-in and the Sunday papers before settling down to watch the TV highlights from the previous day, all over the country a band of men are hard at work preparing for the next home match.

On the face of it, Arsenal, with their famous marble halls and a history taking in over 60 years of unbroken First Division membership and regular appearances at Wembley and in Europe, are light years removed from Halifax Town's cinder-bank terracing and a past which includes three applications for re-election to the League.

But Gordon Ross, who has edited Arsenal's programme for over 31 years, and Tony Thwaites, a comparative novice with more than five years' service on Town's programme, have much in common. Not least their passion for the clubs whose programmes they compile, a devotion which is reflected in the quality of the finished product, despite the obvious gulf in status between the two clubs.

'My big interest has always been cricket,' says Gordon, 'But Arsenal has always meant something very special to me. It's more than just a job – I'm a part of this club. In fact, I'd say my interest is not really in football but in Arsenal. I see very few matches otherwise.'

It's also a labour of love for Tony. Perhaps even more so, since unlike his contemporary at Highbury, he isn't paid for working on the club programme. 'It's always been Halifax Town for me. I used to carry the tea-urns when I was a lad in short pants. I've been a ball-boy and a programme seller at the Shay, and I even had trials here as a schoolboy player.'

The programme editor's job is not particularly glamorous, as Gordon explains. 'As well as being editor for Arsenal, I'm also the

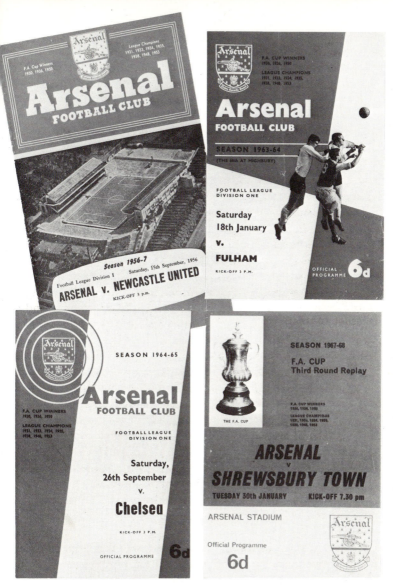

Above: *Four of Gordon Ross's efforts with Arsenal.* **Top left:** *Arsenal v Newcastle United, 1956-57.* **Top right:** *Arsenal v Fulham, 1963-64, which as the cover noted was Arsenal's 50th season at Highbury.* **Above left:** *Arsenal v Chelsea, 1964-65.* **Above right:** *Arsenal v Shrewsbury, FA Cup, 1967-68. This was a 16-page edition, five of them taken up by pictures. As always with Arsenal there was no advertising, and it was only 6d (2½p).*

club's historian. A lot of my work is simply updating the lists of appearances and goalscorers for our first team, reserves and youth team after Saturday's games.'

Gordon writes 'Voice of Arsenal' — the editorial column on the inside front cover, but the programme also contains interviews or articles by guest writers (usually managers, journalists or former players) and a selection of photographs, two pages of which are in full colour. For Halifax, with an average gate of about 2,000 – Arsenal's is nearly 20 times that size – such features are a luxury they simply cannot afford. Instead, Tony Thwaites produces their programme almost single handed.

'I design it and I write or compile everything in it, apart from the manager's column,' he says. 'I first started doing the job about five years back. Originally I did it for love, as a collector and a fan – I suppose I still do – although now I'm working for the club as commercial manager.

'I keep all the facts and figures up to date, write a general piece of the recent results and transfers in our division, and I try to feature the commercial scene too. To a club like Halifax, the lottery is all-important and needs publicising.

'I've also introduced a section called "Swapshop" in which our fans – and anyone else who's interested – can have their programme "wants" advertised free. It has proved very popular, and I've heard of some collectors being sent packages of old programmes free as a result of using the service. One or two other clubs are starting to pick up on the idea, which can only be good news for programme collectors.'

Making sure that the pen-pictures and team photo of the visiting club are interesting and up to date is important to both men.

'A lot of clubs send out a photo and player profiles at the beginning of the season, but I don't tend to use them,' says Gordon Ross. 'By the time Arsenal come to play a particular team, several of those players might have been transferred, not to mention managers leaving. I get an agency in Fleet Street to prepare them for us a few days before the game. There's nothing worse than buying a programme and finding pen-pictures of players who left months before.'

Tony Thwaites tackles the problem in a similarly intelligent fashion. 'The visiting club usually send us pen-pictures a month ahead, but I always rewrite them on the Sunday before to take in

Left: *The Halifax Town programme of 1960-61, when the Shaymen competed in the Third Division along with QPR, Coventry City and Bristol City.* **Above:** *Town's 1978-79 edition, written, edited and designed by Tony Thwaites.*

any transfers, or other new information that might interest our fans.'

On the Monday before a game, while Arsenal's printers are preparing to run off as many as 30,000 programmes, Tony is busy delivering his handwritten 'copy' to Town's printers, who are owned by one of the Halifax board of directors. But that is far from the end of their task. Both Gordon and Tony have to estimate the size of the crowd to give the printers an estimate for the print-run. Three hundred programmes left over at the Shay is a minor disaster, while 2,000 unsold copies causes furrowed brows down Highbury way.

'Our print order depends on several factors,' says Gordon. 'Where Arsenal are in the League table, how we did the previous Saturday, where our opponents are in the table and whether they're likely to bring many supporters with them. When Manchester United, Tottenham or Liverpool come to us, we expect to get close to a sell-out. But without wishing to be unkind to anyone, the Coventrys and Middlesbroughs never seem to attract much of a crowd here.

'The one thing you can never budget for is the weather. If it's freezing cold on the day it can throw your calculation right out. And you must try to make sure you don't under-order. If someone comes along and you've sold out, they're entitled to complain, especially since our programmes contain a voucher which can help towards getting a cup final ticket.'

When Saturday finally comes around, Gordon Ross's task is almost over for another week. When he arrives at the stadium, he checks that the printers have sent the right quantity of programmes. Then, after watching the match from his seat in the main stand, he returns to find out the sales figures for the day.

Meanwhile, up at Halifax, Tony Thwaites arrives at the ground in the morning to take out programmes for people who have subscriptions. He also removes about 100 copies for the visiting club to take back to their club shop. As kick-off time approaches, he turns his attention to Town's eight or nine programme sellers, giving them instructions to surrender their programmes if, as happened once, away supporters threaten violence.

'They're mostly young lads, aged about 14 to 18,' he explains. 'We give them 1p per programme sold, plus free admission to the match and tea and biscuits. They're a grand bunch, and turn up in

Above left: *Arsenal v Real Madrid, 1962-63. Facing Di Stefano, Puskas and Gento in this 'friendly' was Terry Neill.*
Above right: *Bangor City v AC Napoli (Italy), a European Cup Winners Cup first round play-off staged at Arsenal in 1962-63. Napoli finally overcame the Welsh Cup holders' resistance, winning the third game 2-1.*
Left: *Arsenal v Rangers, 1962-63. This was a testimonial for the Gunners' great Welsh international keeper Jack Kelsey.*

all kinds of awful weather.'

The programme editor also has to be on his mettle when his club are drawn away in a cup tie. In 1978 Tony prepared a whole issue which the printers were ready to do a rush job on in case Halifax drew at Carlisle. 'We lost 1-0 to a goal in the 87th minute and never got the replay,' he sighs. 'So you can end up putting four or five hours graft into something that you're never going to use.'

Postponed matches are another bugbear. Arsenal can afford to write off the loss and print an entirely new edition for the rearranged game, unless it can be played the following night so that the statistics are still relevant. Halifax, however, produce a four-page supplement which is wrapped around the original issue.

Gordon Ross is quietly satisfied that Arsenal's programme, which has never carried advertisements, offers value for money and a good read. 'In 1979-80 we had sold over half-a-million copies before December, including 51,000 against Liverpool. So we can't be doing too badly. I occasionally get letters saying we live in the past, but Arsenal are a club with a great history and tradition and I feel the programme shouldn't ignore that.'

Tony Thwaites knows he'll never be able to match Arsenal's figures, but believes that Town's programme is a worthy effort on limited resources. 'Ideally, I'd like us to have colour photos, an action photo spread, and crossword puzzles and competitions to keep the crowd occupied at half-time, and also to give away fans something to do on the train home.'

How do they view the development of football programmes generally? Gordon: 'It's not for me to criticise other clubs, but I don't see Arsenal as a magazine publishing company, nor does the board of directors. We believe in a more traditional club programme, rather than in a magazine full of slick public relations material. Every club has eleven public relations officers – on the field each Saturday.' Tony: 'A programme is a club's link with its fans. If you get too much uniformity in programmes, which is happening now to an extent, then you lose individuality. It should reflect the club, and be their communication with the man on the terraces – those supporters who are the lifeblood of a club like Halifax.'

Not surprisingly, both are keen collectors. Among Gordon's prize possessions is a bound volume of all the Gunners' programmes for the 1926-27 season, while Tony specialises in Halifax

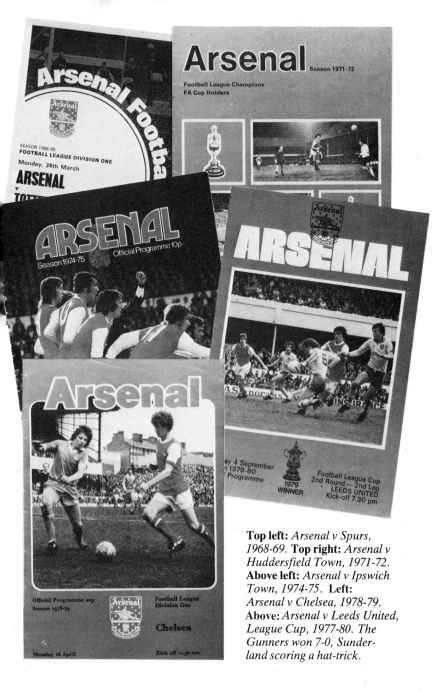

Top left: *Arsenal v Spurs, 1968-69.* **Top right:** *Arsenal v Huddersfield Town, 1971-72.* **Above left:** *Arsenal v Ipswich Town, 1974-75.* **Left:** *Arsenal v Chelsea, 1978-79.* **Above:** *Arsenal v Leeds United, League Cup, 1977-80. The Gunners won 7-0, Sunderland scoring a hat-trick.*

Town programmes, past and present. 'I've got a photostat of a programme from our first season in the League, back in 1921, and some from the 1930s. But the one I've been after for ages is Halifax v Spurs in the fifth round of the FA Cup in 1952-53. I had a copy once, but I lent it to a friend. He emigrated with it!'

So the task of compiling a club programme is neither easy nor glamorous. To bring you an interesting edition every other week for nine months, the editors have to do a lot of hard graft and routine work.

Despite their constant contact with programmes, neither editor gets bored or disillusioned with his job. 'I still get excited when Saturday comes around,' says Gordon. 'When I don't, I suppose that will be the time to call it a day.' Tony agrees: 'If Manchester United came for me to do their programme, I'd probably jump at the chance . . . but only if I could still do Halifax's. I love the club and I enjoy doing the programme – for me it's more like a hobby than a job.'

7: Every Programme Tells A Story

'UNITED WILL GO ON'

Programmes from any match involving Manchester United are always in demand. But one particular edition of the 'United Review' holds a special place in many collections. It is the issue for United's fifth round FA Cup tie against Sheffield Wednesday played on Wednesday, 19th February 1958.

A fortnight earlier the brilliant young United squad – known affectionately as the 'Busby Babes' – had flown out to Belgrade for the second leg of a European Cup tie against Yugoslavian champions Red Star holding a 2-1 lead from the first leg. The game was a real thriller, and United marched into the semi-finals with a 5-4 aggregate victory after a 3-3 draw.

The return flight took in a stop at Munich in West Germany. It was there, on 6 February, that arguably the greatest club football team Britain has every produced was destroyed. In driving snow the team's plane powered through the slush on the runway at over 100 mph, crashed through the boundary fence, struck a tree, then smashed into a house. Of the people on that plane, 21 died on that dark Munich afternoon and two more died later in hospital. Eleven belonged to the club, including England internationals Roger Byrne, Duncan Edwards and Tommy Taylor.

The game for the following Saturday was naturally cancelled as the nation mourned. A week later United were due to play Wednesday in the Cup, but the FA helped by agreeing to postpone the tie for four days to assist Jimmy Murphy, stand-in manager for the critically injured Matt Busby, to scrape a team together. Only two of the Munich survivors, Harry Gregg and Bill Foulkes, were fit to play. Several juniors were called up for their debuts, and two players hastily bought. One of them, Aston Villa's Stan Crowther, was signed just 54 minutes before kick-off and given special permission to play, despite being officially Cup-tied.

United's dilemma is captured perfectly by the team line-ups in

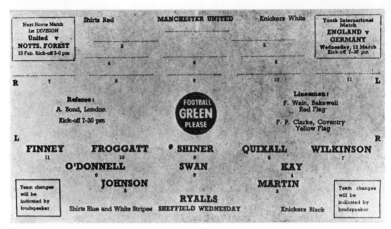

Above: *The bare programme for United's FA Cup tie with Sheffield Wednesday two weeks after the Munich disaster. Remarkably, United's hotch-potch of reserves, third-teamers and hurried buys won 3-0. Stand-in manager Jimmy Murphy commented: 'The players ran themselves to a standstill . . . Poor old Sheffield never had a chance.'*

Above: *The line-ups from the programme of the 'Busby Babes' last match, against Red Star Belgrade in Yugoslavia on 5 February 1958. United had finished the previous two seasons as League champions, and their aggregate win over Red Star took them into their second European Cup semi-final.*

the centre pages of the programme. The Sheffield Wednesday side was printed as normal: but nobody – not even Jimmy Murphy – was sure who would be representing United, and the spaces were left blank for the 60,000 fans to fill in accordingly. In the end a line-up of Harry Gregg, Bill Foulkes, Ian Greaves, Stan Crowther, Ron Cope, Freddie Goodwin, Colin Webster, Ernie Taylor, Alex Dawson, Mark Pearson and Shay Brennan sent an emotional crowd home in triumphant mood after a 3-0 win.

With its black bordered cover, containing a message from the United chairman headed 'United will go on', the programme for this historic match has become a real collectors' item, which even those who had given up the hobby are loath to part with. The Red Star edition from the match in Belgrade is virtually impossible to obtain now, although some copies of the programme from the 'Busby Babes' last match in England – a marvellous 5-4 league victory at Arsenal – are still in circulation.

* * *

CLIVE SEES RED

Did you hear about the player who got the red card for missing an open goal? It happened during the friendly match between Chelsea and Los Angeles Aztecs at Stamford Bridge early in the 1979-80 season. Each programme for the match contained a two-colour card. The idea was that when referee Tony Glasson blew for a foul or spoke to a player, the fans could give their verdict by lifting the red side if they thought the culprit should be sent off or the yellow face if he ought to be booked.

In the event, nobody was actually booked, but that didn't stop Chelsea winger Clive Walker from being shown the red card by the crowd when he wasted a couple of good chances! Despite the presence of Johan Cruyff in the Aztecs team, only 10,000 fans turned up to see Chelsea's 2-0 success. However, all 10,000 programmes printed were sold.

* * *

VOUCHER MADNESS!

More proof, if any were needed, of the extremes to which some Manchester United supporters will go in order to see their team play. When United met Bury in the first round of the Lancashire Youth Cup at Old Trafford in the opening weeks of the 1979-80 season, nearly 14,000 people paid to get into Old Trafford for the game – more than ten times the number such a match would normally have attracted.

The reason? The match programme included a voucher which the fans could use in order to obtain a ticket for the FA Cup final should United reach it. But there are limits even to the fanaticism of the most fervent 'Reds' – most of them left immediately after buying their programme and missed their youth team's 3-0 victory.

* * *

HIGHLAND FLING

One of the most eagerly pursued programmes during the 1978-79 season was the one produced for what looked, on paper, a fairly run-of-the-mill Scottish FA Cup tie between Inverness Thistle of the Highland League and Scottish Second Division outfit Falkirk.

Because of the appalling weather which hit the far north that winter, the tie was postponed 29 times. Falkirk eventually won 4-0, but the non-League club were rewarded with record gate receipts of £784.10 from a crowd of 1,543, and the interest generated by the record number of postponements also resulted in several hundred requests for the official programme, bringing Thistle some very welcome cash.

The previous season Thistle had combined with their neighbours Inverness Caledonian to produce a special issue when the clubs met in a 'derby'. Their efforts were recognised by the Wirral Programme Club in their non-League survey; it was voted 'best special issue'. In 1979-80 the award again went to a Scottish club – Threave Rovers, for their programme for the Scottish Cup first round tie with East Stirlingshire

* * *

THE NAME GAME

The names of British players in the programmes of foreign clubs often make amusing reading. For instance, when West Bromwich Albion visited Red Star Belgrade in the 1978-79 UEFA Cup, the Yugoslavian programme listed the following players; Dzon Vile

Above: *The programme from the match which launched Inverness Thistle to national fame – the Scottish FA Cup tie against Falkirk which, due to snow and ice in the Scottish Highlands in the winter of 1978-79, was postponed no less than 29 times. Thistle's consolation when they lost 4-0 at the 30th attempt was the record sum of nearly £785 taken at the gate.*

(John Wile), i Ville Dzonzton (Willie Johnston) Ali Brovn (Ally Brown) and Syrile Regiz (Cyrille Regis)! Unfortunately the laugh was on Albion, who went down 2-1 on aggregate.

In the programme published by Valletta of Malta for their UEFA Cup first round first leg game against Leeds United in September 1979, the Valletta secretary Freddie Mizzi welcomed Leeds by describing them as 'the backbone of the England side', singling out Tony Currie for special praise. Currie had left Leeds two months earlier for Queen's Park Rangers! To make matter worse, the programme also featured photos of some of the Leeds stars – and among them were David Stewart and Peter Lorimer, both of whom had left Elland Road the previous season. Nonetheless, the Valletta programme is a worthy effort for a small club in one of the game's developing nations, and those few mistakes have perhaps added to its value to collectors.

* * *

RECORD-BREAKING REDS

You just can't keep Manchester United's name out of it when discussing programmes. The Old Trafford club claim three Foot-

Above: *Two of the highest-selling club programmes of all time – Manchester United v Estudiantes, 1968-69, and v Real Madrid, 1967-68.*

ball League records for match programme sales: the highest figure for any match other than a cup final – 74,680 copies sold when they met Estudiantes de la Plata of Argentina for the World Cup Championship in 1968, the record for a Football League game – 64,772 copies sold for the clash with Arsenal, also in 1968-69; and the best figure for a European match (non-final) – 60,462 copies sold for the meeting with Real Madrid in the semi-final of the 1967-68 European Championships Cup.

* * *

THE SHAPE OF PROGRAMMES TO COME?

The growth in the popularity of soccer in the United States has sparked an enormous amount of interest outside that country, and nowhere more so than in Britain, which has supplied more players to the North American Soccer League (NASL) than any other country.

NASL matches do not have programmes as we know them. Instead, there is a magazine called 'Kick', which is on sale at every stadium. The NASL's marketing division in New York City produces the bulk of the magazine, commissioning general interest articles and securing advertising. These are then printed up and flown out to the League's 24 clubs, who produce an insert of the same page-size and typeface which is then inserted into 'Kick'. This section, which varies in size according to the support and the volume of advertising the clubs attract, contains local news and photos as well as the team line-ups for that day.

This means that all NASL matches on any one day have essentially the same programme, whether they are played in Boston or 3,000 miles away in San Francisco. Although 389 matches are played in the NASL between March and September, only 19 issues of 'Kick' are produced – 15 for each club's home matches, three for the play-offs and one for the Soccer Bowl, the season's grand finale.

So the only programme for a specific match is the 'Kick' published for the Soccer Bowl, the match between the two clubs who go through from the play-offs to meet in New Jersey's Giants Stadium (home of the Cosmos) for the right to be called Champions of North America. The 1979 final, between Rodney Marsh's Tampa Bay Rowdies and Alan Ball's Vancouver Whitecaps, had a

Above: *The impressive silver, blue and red cover of the edition of 'Kick' produced by the North American Soccer League for the Soccer Bowl '79, when Vancouver Whitecaps met Tampa Bay Rowdies in New Jersey. Whitecaps won 2-1, both their goals coming from Trevor Whymark, the former Ipswich and England striker who returned to play for Derby in the 1979-80 season. Willie Johnston and skipper Alan Ball were among his Vancouver team-mates.*

114-page edition featuring several lengthy features on the key players and the rival coaches, plus a glossary of referees' signals and a potted history of the competition.

The differences in the approach to the game between Britain and the USA are clearly illustrated by the pen pictures of the Soccer Bowl finalists. Rowdies' Manny Andruszewski is described as 'very defensive minded . . . attempted only 11 shots in 1,345 minutes of action', and his team-mate John Gorman is noted for 'commiting only 26 fouls in 2,469 minutes'. For the Whitecaps, defender Bob Bolitho is listed as having 'registered four assists in one match, the only full-back in the NASL ever to do so', while midfielder Bob Lenarduzzi's main claim to fame is that he 'scored in both shootouts last week to eliminate Cosmos'.

Unlike most things American – for example T-shirts, badges and star-spangled soccer balls – the NASL's match-day magazine has failed to prove very popular with British fans. As one programme editor put it: 'They're too standardised . . . see one and you've seen them all. British programmes have gone that way to an extent, with several clubs using the same designers or printers, but I hope it never comes down to one programme to cover every League match on one day.' And at another club, the shop manager commented: 'We got some copies of "Kick" in, thinking they would be a good seller, but they proved very unpopular. The fans seem to prefer the traditional programme.'

* * *

THE MANAGER WHO WASN'T

Leeds United were jumping the gun somewhat when they greeted 'Our New Manager' in their programme against Blackburn Rovers on 11 April 1959. The editorial stated 'Our new manager is 50-year-old Mr Arthur Turner, the former Birmingham City "chief" who took the St Andrews side to the FA Cup final of 1956 . . .'. The announcement turned out to be premature: Turner stayed with his Southern League Club, Headington United, who changed their name to Oxford United, and gained entrance to the Football League within three years under Turner's guidance.

In the end Jack Taylor was appointed to the Leeds job, but listed at number 10 for the Peacocks in that Blackburn programme was the name of the man who eventually led them to success at home and in Europe – Don Revie, then in the later stages of an illustrious playing career. Incidentally, at number 11 for Rovers that day was another player who went on to become manager of his country's national team, Ally MacLeod.

* * *

THE 'PENNY BLACK' OF PROGRAMMES

Probably the most sought-after programme is the issue, priced 3d in 'old' money, for the first FA Cup final ever played at Wembley, the match between Bolton Wanderers and West Ham United in 1923. Bolton won 2-0, but the match is best remembered for the fact that a crowd estimated at over 150,000 saw it, many of them having broken gates down to gain entrance, and also for the appearance of a policeman on a white horse who tried to control the crowds. The Football Association were forced to refund £2,797 to ticket holders who had been unable to take their seats!

Wembley Stadium Ltd have produced an exact reproduction of the programme from the 1923 final. Although clearly nowhere near as valuable as an original copy, it makes fascinating reading. There are 28 pages, containing detailed histories, pen-pictures and team-photos of both clubs, and a potted history of the competition itself since its inception in 1871-72.

Like the reproduction of the 1949 final between Wolves and Leicester published by Wolves, it makes no attempt to deceive collectors into thinking they are buying an original, and indeed is clearly marked 'reproduction'. However, 'fakes' of the 1958 final between Bolton and Manchester United are in circulation and are recognisable by the fact that whoever published them broke one of the golden rules of programme collecting by writing the figure '2' on his original copy under the name of the Wanderers centre-forward Nat Lofthouse. This was presumably a way of recording the two goals with which Lofthouse clinched the Cup for Bolton. Unfortunately, he omitted to erase this number when printing the 'fake', and there it is on every copy. Nevertheless, many collectors have bought the programme, believing it to be an 'original'. There is unfortunately no way of spotting the 'fake' by looking at the cover, so check the team line-ups carefully if you're offered one.

Incidentally, original copies of the 1923 final may sell for over £70 if in good condition.

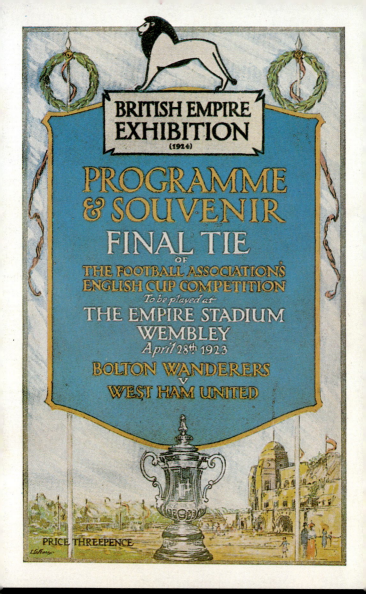

*Above: **The first Wembley FA Cup final, between Bolton Wanderers and West Ham United in 1923. An exact reproduction is available, but an original copy in good condition is becoming increasingly rare.***

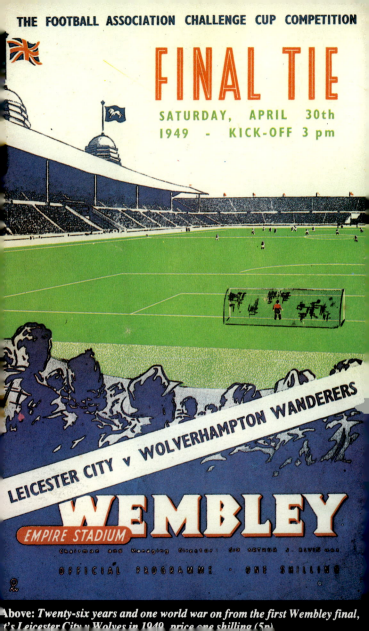

Above: Twenty-six years and one world war on from the first Wembley final, it's Leicester City v Wolves in 1949, price one shilling (5p).

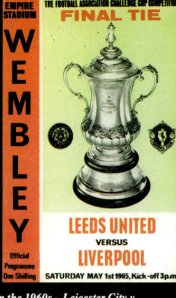

Above: FA Cup final programmes from the 1960s – Leicester City v Manchester United (1963) and Leeds United v Liverpool (1965).

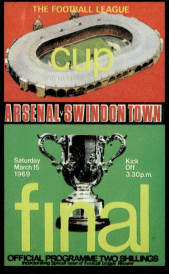

Above: Wembley was the venue for these League Cup finals – Arsenal v Swindon Town (1969) and Manchester City v WBA (1970).

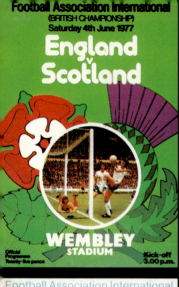

Top left: *England v Scotland at Wembley in the 1977 Home International Championship, when the Scots won 2-1.* **Top right:** *Scotland v Bulgaria at Hampden, only months before Ally MacLeod led his squad in the disastrous World Cup campaign in Argentina.* **Above left:** *England v Hungary at Wembley in 1978, when the Argentina-bound Hungarians lost 4-1.* **Above:** *A colourful Wembley cover for England v Wales in 1979.*

Above: *The programme from the greatest day in English soccer history – the 1966 World Cup final between England and West Germany at Wembley, when England became world champions by winning 4-2 after extra time. This was the only programme produced for a specific match during the tournament: one programme was printed to cover all the group matches, quarter-finals and semi-finals.*

Above: *And now for something completely different . . . when Dutch champions Ajax met Benfica of Portugal in the European Cup quarter-final in 1968-69, the cover had a cartoon depicting Benfica's brilliant striker Eusebio. However, it was Ajax who won the tie.*

Top left: *Atletico Madrid v Fiorentina, Hampden 1962.* **Top right:** *West Ham v TSV Munich, Wembley 1965, when the Hammers won 2-0.* **Above left:** *Hamburg v AC Milan at the Feyenoord Stadium in Holland, 1968.* **Above:** *Ajax v AC Milan, the 1969 European Cup final played in Madrid.*

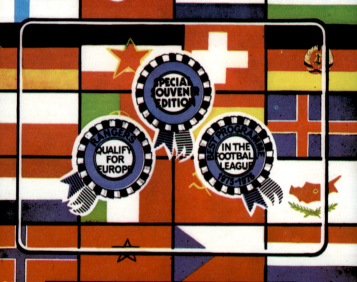

Above: *Queen's Park Rangers celebrated their achievement in qualifying for Europe in 1975-76 with this special edition for their final home match, against Leeds United. Rangers won 2-0.*

ALL CHANGE AT DERBY

When the Baseball Ground fans opened up their programmes before the Derby County v Leeds United clash on Easter Monday 1970, they had no idea of the shock in store for them. There, on the centre spread, was the Leeds line-up which was chasing the treble of League Championship, FA Cup and European Cup: Gary Sprake, Paul Reaney, Terry Cooper, Billy Bremner, Jack Charlton, Norman Hunter, Peter Lorimer, Allan Clarke, Mick Jones, Johnny Giles, Paul Madeley. Sub: Eddie Gray. Every one a household name.

Then half-an-hour before kick-off, with over 41,000 fans packed inside the ground, came the announcement. 'Here are today's programme changes. For Derby Durban moves from 7 to 4, Hennessey switches from 4 to 6, and Wignall comes in at number 7'. No great surprises there – but then the announcer continued: 'For Leeds, David Harvey is in goal, Nigel Davey is at 2, Paul Peterson 3, Jimmy Lumsden 4, David Kennedy 5, Terry Yorath 6, Chris Galvin 7, Mick Bates 8, Rod Belfitt 9, Terry Hibbitt 10, Albert Johanneson 11, and the sub is Sean O'Neill.' It was the complete Leeds reserve side, and although players like Yorath and Harvey later became internationals, the Leeds youngsters were no match for the Rams that day, Derby winning 4-1.

Don Revie, the Leeds manager, had decided to rest his first team in view of the heavy programme facing them in the days ahead. Not only did the defeat effectively end United's pursuit of Everton at the top of Division 1, but Leeds were later fined by the FA for deliberately fielding a weakened side.

* * *

LEAGUE NEW BOYS

The programme from the very first League game ever played by a club always has particular value. Since 1970 Cambridge United, Hereford United, Wimbledon and Wigan Athletic have all gained admission. Cambridge began with a home game, but Hereford were away, while Wimbledon and Wigan had both played, as League members, in the first round of the Football League Cup before their opening Fourth Division fixture.

Here are the programmes to watch out for:
Cambridge United v Lincoln City, Division 4, 15 August 1970.

Colchester United v **Hereford United**, Division 4, 12 August 1972. (first home v Reading, Division 4, 19 August 1972).
Wimbledon v Halifax Town, Division 4, 20 August 1977. (Wimbledon had met Gillingham twice in the League Cup before this, away on 13 August 1977 and at home on 16 August 1977).
Hereford United v **Wigan Athletic**, Division 4, 19 August 1978. (Wigan had met Tranmere twice in the League Cup before this, away on 12 August 1978 and at home on 16 August 1978; their first home match in the League was v Grimsby Town, Division 4, 23 August 1978).

* * *

END OF THE ROAD FOR AVENUE

You won't find that name of Bradford Park Avenue in any set of football results today, yet their programmes are among the most popular of all ex-members of the Football League.

As recently as 1950 Bradford were playing in the Second Division against the likes of Spurs, Leeds and West Ham. However, in 1967-68 they won only four of their 46 Fourth Division matches, and for four successive seasons they ended up in the League's bottom four – the last three times in 92nd place. In 1970 the League's AGM voted in Cambridge United, and 51 seasons of League soccer were over for Bradford Park Avenue.

Bradford joined the Northern Premier League immediately, but enjoyed little success their either. For 1973-74 they shared Valley Parade with Bradford City, but with debts mounting and support dwindling, the club was finally wound up at the end of that season.

For most of the 1960s, Park Avenue's programmes were predominantly green, reflecting the club's white and green kit. For several seasons they published a pocket-sized programme (110mm x 140mm), one of which sported a drawing of the distinctive pavilion in which the teams used to change. In their last few League seasons the club switched to a white strip with red and yellow facings. The programme, by now larger (142mm x 220mm), had a glossy cover coloured accordingly.

Bradford persisted with the same cover design in the Northern Premier League until their financial position forced them to change to an altogether plainer black and white edition.

Programmes to look out for are the final home edition in the

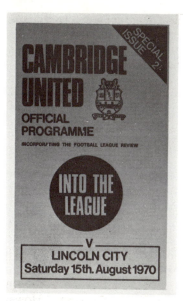

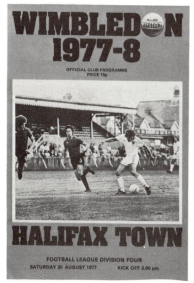
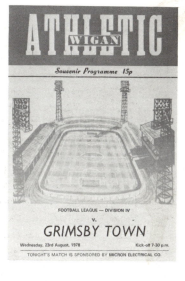

Above: *The first Football League programmes ever published by Cambridge United (v Lincoln, 1970-71), Hereford United (v Reading, 1972-73), Wimbledon (v Halifax, 1977-78) and Wigan Athletic (v Grimsby Town, 1978-79). Of the four, only Wigan lost their first home fixture.*

Football League, for the match against Scunthorpe (which Avenue lost 5-0) on 4 April 1970, and their very last League match, away to Aldershot on 20 April 1970. The club's last-ever programme was for the NPL game with Great Harwood in 1973-74, at Valley Parade.

* * *

SCOTTISH SNIPS

The last Scottish League club to go out of existence was the Glasgow team Third Lanark, who resigned from the competition at the end of 1966-67 despite finishing 11th in the Second Division. Poor crowds and mounting debts meant that this once-proud club – Scottish Cup winners twice and League champions once in their 95-year history – didn't publish any programmes in their final two seasons. The last programme produced for a game featuring Third Lanark is believed to be the one for their away match at Brechin City on 22 April 1967.

Three other Scottish clubs whose programmes you should look out for are those of East Stirlingshire Clydebank, the short-lived amalgamation of East Stirlingshire and Clydebank which competed in the Scottish Second Division in 1964-65, coming fifth; Clydebank, who joined the League in their own right in 1966-67; and Meadowbank Thistle, the Edinburgh club known as Ferranti Thistle until they won election to the Scottish League in 1974-75.

The first programme published by Meadowbank under the new name was a four-pager for the League Cup tie at Meadowbank Stadium on 9 August 1974, against Albion Rovers. Close examination reveals that the name Ferranti Thistle has been overprinted with a black strip on the amber cover, while inside the spaces headed 'Today's Teams' and 'Club Notes' are left blank. Instead, a sheet with teams and notes was inserted.

The club's first home match in the Scottish League was against Stranraer three weeks later, but it seems that the club wasn't quite prepared for the occasion and the home game against Alloa Athletic on 11 September 1974 was regarded as their first 'real' home game. A special 12-page souvenir programme was produced, but sadly Thistle couldn't mark the occasion with a win. They lost 1-0, the fourth in a terrible opening run of nine successive defeats.

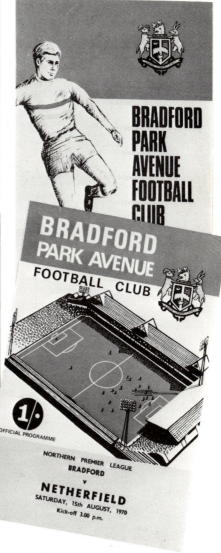

Left: *Three of the mini-programmes issued by Bradford in the 1960s.* **Top:** *The design from Avenue's penultimate Football League season, 1968-69.* **Above:** *Their first NPL edition in 1970-71, against Netherfield.*

Above: *'Hi-Hi News'* – a programme published by the now-defunct Third Lanark club for a Scottish League Division 1 match against Kilmarnock in 1962-63. Within four years the Glasgow club had folded.

E.S. CLYDEBANK

Saturday, 5th September, 1964

Kick-off 3 p.m. at Kilbowie

Scottish League

E.S. CLYDEBANK
VERSUS
DUMBARTON

OFFICIAL PROGRAMME
3d.

Derry City Football & Athletic Club, Ltd.

REGENT

for peak pulling power
it scores every time

Saturday, 27th January, 1962
KICK-OFF 2.45 p.m.

v. ARDS

Official Programme - - - 6d

MEADOWBANK THISTLE
v
ALLOA ATHLETIC

Official Programme
Souvenir Issue

Wednesday September 11·1974

Kick·off 7·30p.m. 10p

Above left: *An East Stirlingshire – Clydebank programme from 1964-65 – for the 'derby' with Dumbarton.*

Above: *Happier days for Irish League club Derry City. This programme is for a match at their Brandywell ground against Ards in 1961-62. Due to the 'troubles' in Ulster, the club were forced to withdraw from the Irish League in 1970s.*

Left: *The official souvenir programme from Meadowbank Thistle's big night. Before joining the Scottish League they were known as Ferranti Thistle and played in the East of Scotland League. With Hearts and Hibs nearby, Meadowbank often play before less than 200 fans.*

'WE'LL MEET AGAIN . . .'

Before Bradford Park Avenue, the last clubs to lose their League status were Gateshead and Accrington Stanley. In fact both were forced out of existence at one stage, but recent years have seen a mini-revival in both areas with the formation of new clubs carrying on the old names.

The new Gateshead play in the Gateshead Stadium made famous by super athlete Brendan Foster, and their 22-page programme for 1978-79 was highly rated by the Wirral Programme Club's annual survey. The re-formed Accrington Stanley club's edition for the same season bore the slogan *'One of football's oldest names'* on its cover – a reference to the fact that Accrington were one of the Football League's 12 founder members back in April 1888.

By a strange coincidence Accrington Stanley and Gateshead, by now playing in the Cheshire League and the Northern Premier League respectively, were drawn together in the FA Trophy in 1978-79 at Stanley's Crown Ground. The programme notes commented that this was the clubs' first meeting in Accrington since 1957 when Stanley won 3-0 in a Third Division North game at their old ground, Peel Park, before a crowd of 6,818. This time a few hundred spectators saw Accrington win 6-1.

* * *

MAKING A FRESH START

Always in demand are the old programmes of clubs who have either changed their names or moved to new grounds.

The last four clubs to alter their names are Orient, who were known as Leyton Orient until the start of the 1967-68 season; Swansea City, who were Swansea Town until February 1970; AFC Bournemouth, known as Bournemouth & Boscombe Athletic until the beginning of 1972-73; and Hartlepool United, who played as Hartlepools United (with an 's') until 1968, then became plain Hartlepool, and turned to their present name in 1977-78.

Since the Second World War, four clubs have switched grounds on a permanent basis, although one later decided they were mistaken and moved back to their old stadium. That club was Queen's Park Rangers, who left Rangers Stadium in South Africa Road midway through 1962-63 for the White City Stadium a few

The programmes of four Football League clubs whose names have changed – Hartlepools United, Leyton Orient, Bournemouth & Boscombe Athletic and Swansea Town.

hundred yards down the road, but returned within a year.

Hull City moved to new premises at Boothferry Park at the start of 1946-47, after playing for 41 years at Anlaby Road, home of Hull Cricket Club. Port Vale left the Recreation Ground in Hanley (known affectionately to the locals as 'the owd wreck') for a brand new stadium in nearby Burslem, which was opened at the start of 1950-51. For a few seasons Vale's programme cover reflected the club's development, depicting the club's first-ever ground – at Limekiln Lane in an area called Longport – alongside an artist's impression of the new ground, Vale Park. Finally, Southend United vacated the old Southend Stadium at the end of 1954-55 and have played at Roots Hall ever since.

* * *

OFF WITH HIS HEAD!

Has football become too serious, with players afraid to make mistakes because of the financial losses they might entail? This clip from the Leeds United programme of 15 December 1945, when Sheffield United were the visitors, suggests that this attitude is nothing new:

'Should players be fined for missing penalty kicks and corner kicks put behind the goal? The ideal placing of a corner kick is just outside the goal area, yet players will try to drop the ball straight into the goalmouth and so play into the hands of the defending side. The ideal place for the penalty is AT THE BACK OF THE NET!

* * *

THE '100 CLUB'

Several clubs have chalked up 100 years or more of existence, and they have invariably marked the occasion by staging a prestigious 'centenary' match, for which a special programme full of fascinating historical material has been produced.

Notts County were the first to reach the 'ton', in 1962, and they played an England XI to celebrate. Stoke City came next, meeting the fabulous Real Madrid side at the Victoria Ground in 1963 when, incidentally, they also won the Second Division title.

Since then Nottingham Forest (1965), Chesterfield (1966),

Above: *The Port Vale programme for 1953-54, one of the first seasons at Vale Park, when they reached the FA Cup semi-final as a Division 3 club.*

Sheffield Wednesday (1967), Reading (1971), Wrexham (1973) Bolton Wanderers and Aston Villa (1974), Birmingham City and Blackburn Rovers (1975), Middlesbrough and Port Vale (1976), Crewe Alexandra, Ipswich Town and Wolves (1977), Grimsby Town and Manchester United (1978), Doncaster Rovers, Fulham, Sunderland and West Bromwich Albion (all 1979) have reached that milestone.

For their centenary, Villa played Leeds United (then the reigning League champions) on 7 August 1974. Included inside the programme was an exact reproduction of the very first edition of the 'Villa News & Record', for the match against Blackburn Rovers on 1 September 1906.

Next in line for membership of soccer's '100 Club'? – Orient, Swindon Town and Preston North End (1981), Burnley, Newcastle and Tottenham Hotspur (1982) and Bristol Rovers, Coventry City, Darlington, Lincoln City, Stockport County and Tranmere Rovers a year later.

* * *

NON-LEAGUE WINNERS

The vast improvement in the contents of football programmes over the past decade has not merely been confined to Football League clubs. Non-League programmes have developed in recent years from advert-packed team-sheets with little editorial matter and no apparent thought to design into highly informative, attractive efforts worthy of a place in any collection.

The Wirral Programme Club has for several years conducted an annual survey of non-League programmes. The results for 1978-79 were as follows:

1st   Farnborough Town (Berger Isthmian League, Division 2).
2nd   Andover (Southern League, Division 1 South).
3rd   Northwood (Hellenic League).

The formation of the Alliance Premier League in 1979-80 saw a further improvement in non-League issues. This League is composed of 20 former members of the Southern League and the Northern Premier League, and hopes eventually to secure automatic promotion to and relegation from the Fourth Division of the Football League. With a bright, progressive image almost as important as a good playing record, it's no surprise that the

PORT VALE FOOTBALL CLUB
CENTENARY CELEBRATION MATCH

1876 — 1976

PORT VALE VERSUS **STOKE CITY**
VALE PARK, MONDAY, 26th APRIL, 1976. KICK-OFF AT 7-30 p.m.
OFFICIAL SOUVENIR PROGRAMME... **15P**

CENTENARY
CELEBRATION
MATCH
1863-1963

STOKE CITY v REAL MADRID

WEDNESDAY, 24th APRIL, 1963   Price: ONE SHILLING

The two Stoke-on-Trent clubs were among the first to reach their centenary. **Left:** *Stoke City celebrated with a game against Real Madrid in 1962-63. The Potters held their illustrious visitors to a 2-2 draw in front of 44,914 spectators.* **Above:** *Thirteen years later Stoke did the honours as their neighbours Port Vale completed 100 years. This time fewer than 10,000 turned up to mark the occasion and saw a 1-1 draw.*

programmes of several Alliance clubs are excellent.

For the addresses of APL clubs, write to The Press Officer, Alliance Premier League, 129 Haig Avenue, Southport, Lancs. Remember to send a stamped, self-addressed envelope.

* * *

'PROGRAMME OF THE YEAR' AWARDS

The British Programme Club began annual awards for the best club programme in 1965-66, with members voting on the basis of size, price, cover design, articles and the use of photographs. Since 1976-77, the Commercial Managers' Association have been making the selection by setting up a panel of printers, journalists and, of course, commercial managers from League clubs.

The list of winners to date is as follows:

1965-66	Arsenal
1966-67	Chelsea
1967-68	Coventry City
1968-69	Coventry City
1969-70	Chelsea
1970-71	Aston Villa
1971-72	Aston Villa
1972-73	Aston Villa
1973-74	Leeds United
1974-75	Leeds United
1975-76	Queen's Park Rangers
1976-77	Aston Villa
1977-78	Aston Villa
1978-79	West Bromwich Albion

Top left: *New Brighton, Cheshire League, 1966-67. Until 1951 they were members of the Third Division (North).* **Top right:** *Stalybridge Celtic, Cheshire League, 1966-67. Stalybridge also played in the old Third (North). Ironically, they were replaced in 1923 by New Brighton.* **Above:** *The famous North-Eastern amateur club Bishop Auckland – a programme from the FA Amateur Cup, 1961-62.* **Left:** *Isthmian League club Farnborough Town's award-winning 1978-79 edition.*

Above: *Burton Albion v Whitwick Colliery, Birmingham League, 1955-56. Burton later joined the Southern League and now compete in the NPL.*

8: Directory of Football League Programmes

A club-by-club guide to help you get the programmes you want from the 92 Football League clubs – where to write for annual subscriptions or for copies from particular matches plus information about club shops. Always remember to enclose a stamped addressed envelope: a small one will suffice for subscription details, but to avoid unnecessary folding you should send a large envelope when writing for programmes. Envelopes measuring 306mm x 229mm will fit most programmes, although where a programme is listed as having a newspaper format you should try to send an even larger one. Prices correct for the 1979/80 season.

ALDERSHOT
Price: 20p.
Seasonal subscription: write to The General Office, Aldershot FC Ltd, Recreation Ground, High St, Aldershot GU11, Hants.
Individual copies: as above.
Club shop: Supporters Club Shop at ground, open match days only.

ARSENAL
Price: 20p.
Seasonal subscription: write for details to The Gunners Shop, Arsenal FC Ltd, Arsenal Stadium, Avenell Rd, London N5.
Individual copies: as above.
Club shop: as above, open weekdays 9.30-4.45 and on match days; most homes and aways available.
Extra information: the Arsenal programme contains a colour centre spread and no advertisements.

ASTON VILLA
Price: 30p (called 'Villa News & Record').
Seasonal subscription: details from The General Office, Aston Villa, Villa Park, Trinity Rd, Birmingham B6 6HE.
Individual copies: write to Gerald Harris Associates, 550 Chester Rd, Aldridge, West Midlands WS9 0LM.
Club shop: adjacent to ground, open weekdays (except Mondays) 9.30-4.45 and on match days; good selection of programmes.

BARNSLEY
Price: 20p.
Seasonal subscription: details from The General Office, Barnsley FC Ltd, Oakwell Ground, Grove St, Barnsley, Yorks.
Individual copies: as above.
Club shop: two inside the ground, open match days only.

BIRMINGHAM CITY
Price: 25p (called 'Birmingham City News').
Seasonal subscription: details from John Garrard, The Midland Programme Shop, 253 Oxhill Rd, Handsworth, Birmingham.
Individual copies: as above.
Club shop: The Beautique, 26 Cattell Rd, Birmingham 9; open weekdays 9.30-5.30 and on match days; good selection of programmes including Birmingham aways.

BLACKBURN ROVERS
Price: 20p.
Seasonal subscription: not available.
Individual copies: write to The Club Shop, Blackburn Rovers FC Ltd, Ewood Park, Blackburn BB2 4JF, Lancs.
Club shop: as above; open Monday, Tuesday, Thursday and Friday 10.00-5.30, Wednesday 10.00-1.00 and on match days; Rovers aways available.

BLACKPOOL
Price: 20p (called 'The Seasider').
Seasonal subscription: write for details to Sportscene Promotions Ltd, The Refuge Assurance Building, Ainsworth St, Blackburn BB1 6AZ, Lancs.
Individual copies: as above.
Club shop: Blackpool FC Shop, Bloomfield Rd, Blackpool FY1 6JJ, Lancs; open weekdays 9.00-5.00 and on match days; most aways available.
Extra information: Blackpool are one of six clubs whose programmes for 1979-80 were produced by a Blackburn firm, Sportscene Ltd, in a newspaper format.

BOLTON WANDERERS
Price: 20p.
Seasonal subscription: write for details to 'The Happy Shop', Bolton Wanderers FC Ltd, Burnden Park, Bolton BL3 2QR, Lancs.
Individual copies: as above.
Club shop: as above; open weekdays 10.00-5.00 (not Wednesdays) and on match days.

AFC BOURNEMOUTH
Price: 25p (called 'The Cherry Bee').
Seasonal subscription: write to The Cherry Bees Shop, AFC

Above: *The Villa v Walsall Third Division 'derby' from 1971-72, when British Programme Club members voted Villa's 'News & Record' into top spot.* **Left:** *Blackpool v Spurs, 1956-57, when the Lancashire club were still members of Division 1.*

Bournemouth Ltd, Dean Court, Bournemouth BH7 7AF, Dorset.
Individual copies: as above.
Club shop: as above; open match days, although it will be opened on weekdays if you ask at the club offices.
Extra information: Bournemouth's programme is one of the best in the League, with a comprehensive section on the visiting team, good action photos and a historical feature called 'Scrapbook'. Also contains 'On Target' colour supplement.

BRADFORD CITY
Price: 20p.
Seasonal subscription: not available.
Individual copies: write to The City Shop, Bradford City FC Ltd, Valley Parade, Bradford BD8 7DY, West Yorkshire.
Club shop: as above; open match days, although it will be opened if you call at the club office on weekdays.

BRENTFORD
Price: 30p.
Seasonal subscription: not available.
Individual copies: write to The Club Shop, Brentford FC Ltd, Griffin Park, Braemar Rd, Brentford, Middlesex TW8 0NT.
Club shop: as above; open on match days only.
Extra information: Brentford sell a programme to more than 50% of their average home crowd.

BRIGHTON & HOVE ALBION
Price: 20p.
Seasonal subscription: write to The Albion Shop, Brighton & Hove Albion FC Ltd, Goldstone Ground, Hove, Sussex BN3 7DE.
Individual copies: as above.
Club shop: as above; open weekdays 9.00-5.00 and on match days; limited selection of aways available.
Extra information: In 1977-78, Brighton sold a programme to 33% of their average home crowd ; in 1978-79, when they were promoted, the figure rose to 42%, and in the First Division in 1979-80, it was up to more than 50%.

BRISTOL CITY
Price: 30p (called 'The Robin').
Seasonal subscription: write to Sports Projects Ltd, 100 Wigorn Rd, Smethwick, Warley, West Midlands B67 5HL.
Individual copies: as above, or from The City Shop, Bristol City FC Ltd, Ashton Gate, Bristol BS3 2EJ.
Club shop: as above, open weekdays 10.00-5.00 and on match days. Good selection of programmes available, including City aways.
Extra information: Before 1979-80, the club programme was called 'City News'. It was then taken over by a Midlands firm, who also produce the

Above: *It's the Fourth Division against the Isthmian League as AFC Bournemouth take on Hitchin in the first round of the FA Cup in 1978-79. The League side won 2-1 on this occasion, but the Isthmian League proved its strength the next season when Barking and Harlow knocked out League opponents, Croydon held Millwall, and non-League Chesham also reached the third round. Number 8 for Bournemouth against Hitchin was Ted MacDougall, who in 1971-72 scored a record nine goals in Bournemouth's 11-0 Cup win over Margate.*

Norwich programme; it has a different full colour cover each issue and contains no adverts.

BRISTOL ROVERS
Price: 25p.
Seasonal subscription: not available.
Individual copies: write to The Rovers Shop, 468 Stapleton Rd, Bristol 5.
Club shop: as above; open weekdays 9.30-5.30 and match days; programmes from all Rovers aways available.
Extra information: Rovers' programme sells to over 50% of their average home crowd, a high figure probably due to its excellent pictorial and statistical content and the fact that it contains only one page of advertising.

BURNLEY
Price: 25p (called 'The Claret').
Seasonal subscription: write for details to The Claret & Blue Shop, Burnley FC Ltd, Brunshaw Rd, Burnley, Lancs BB10 4BX.
Individual copies: as above.
Club shop: as above; open match days, although it will also be opened for callers to the Development Office (also in Brunshaw Rd).

BURY
Price: 20p (called 'The Shakers' Review').
Seasonal subscription: not available.
Individual copies: write to The Club Secretary, Bury FC Ltd, Gigg Lane, Bury BL9 9HR, Lancs.
Club shop: The Souvenir Shop at the ground is open on match days only.

CAMBRIDGE UNITED
Price: 25p
Seasonal subscription: write for details to Mr D. Arliss, Cambridge United FC Ltd, Abbey Stadium, Newmarket Rd, Cambridge.
Individual copies: as above.
Club shop: there are two, one at the main entrance, the other in the ground, both open on match days and with a good selection of United's aways.
Extra information: The club did experiment with a newspaper format for a while, but for the 1979-80 season they were back to a more traditional type of programme. The club claimed a 66% sale for Second Division matches in 1979-80.

CARDIFF CITY
Price: 20p.
Seasonal subscription: write for details to The Promotions Office, Cardiff City FC Ltd, Ninian Park, Cardiff CF1 8SX.
Individual copies: as above.
Club shop: The Bluebirds Shop at the ground is open on match days only.

Above: *Burnley v Reims in the European Champions Cup, 1960-61. After beating the French champions, Burnley went out to SV Hamburg.*

CARLISLE UNITED
Price: 20p.
Seasonal subscription: write for details to The Secretary, Carlisle United FC Ltd, Brunton Park, Carlisle, Cumbria.
Individual copies: as above.
Club shop: The Supporters Club run a programme shop from a caravan at the ground on match days, specialising in the club's away games.

CHARLTON ATHLETIC
Price: 25p.
Seasonal subscription: write for details to The Commercial Manager, Charlton Athletic FC Ltd, The Valley, Floyd Rd, London SE7.
Individual copies: as above.
Club shop: The Valley Shop, at ground; behind main stand, open match days only.
Extra information: programme binders available from above address.

CHELSEA.
Price: 25p.
Seasonal subscription: write for details to The General Office, Chelsea FC Ltd, Stamford Bridge, Fulham Rd, London SW6.
Individual copies: as above.
Club shop: there is a programme shop inside the ground, by the main entrance, open match days only; the Supporters Club runs a programme shop at 547 Fulham Rd, SW6, and programmes from most Chelsea aways are on sale at both.
Extra information: The Chelsea programme has maintained a high standard for so long, that the fact that they sell to 80% of their average crowd comes as no surprise. The club also reports regular sell-outs, despite fluctuating fortunes in recent seasons.

CHESTER
Price: 20p (called 'Seals Scene').
Seasonal subscription: not available.
Individual copies: write to Chester FC, The Georgian House, Grosvenor St, Chester, Cheshire.
Club shop: as above; open weekdays. All Chester's aways available.
Extra information: Chester's programme for 1979-80 was a drastic improvement on previous years' efforts, which the club's commercial manager describes as 'diabolical'. Contains 'On Target' supplement.

CHESTERFIELD
Price: 15p.
Seasonal subscription: not available.
Individual copies: write to The Club Shop, Chesterfield FC Ltd, Saltergate, Chesterfield, Derbyshire.
Club shop: as above; match days only, with limited supply of the club's aways available.

COLCHESTER UNITED
Price: 25p.
Seasonal subscription: write for details to The Development Department, Colchester United FC Ltd, Layer Rd, Colchester.
Individual copies: as above.
Club shop: at the ground, open match days only.

COVENTRY CITY
Price: 30p (called 'The Sky Blue').
Seasonal subscription: write for details to Programme Subscriptions, Coventry City FC Ltd, Highfield Rd, Coventry.
Individual copies: as above.
Club shop: 'The Sky Blue Shop' in Thackhall St (adjacent to the stadium) is open weekdays 9.00-5.30, and another shop opens on match days in the main stand. Both have a good stock of programmes.
Extra information: Perhaps surprisingly for the club which pioneered the match-day magazine. Coventry's programme for 1979-80 contained the 'Programme Plus' supplement. Current average sale is around 50%.

CREWE ALEXANDRA
Price: 20p.
Seasonal subscription: enquiries to Mr H. Finch (Programme Editor) c/o Crewe Alexandra FC Ltd, Gresty Rd, Crewe, Cheshire.
Individual copies: as above.
Club shop: the club now runs a Programme Shop at 70 Gresty Rd, stocking a wide range of clubs and Crewe aways; open weekday lunchtimes 1.00-2.00 and match days.
Extra information: The 1979-80 edition contained a good spread of action photos. Also contained 'On Target' supplement.

CRYSTAL PALACE
Price: 25p.
Seasonal subscription: write to The General Office, Crystal Palace FC Ltd, Selhurst Park, London SE25.
Individual copies: as above.
Club shop: Main shops at ground are open weekdays 9.00-5.00, but they tend not to stock many programmes; however, there is a programme shop by the old stand, open match days only.
Extra information: In common with most London supporters, Palace fans are keen programme buyers; even in the Third Division in 1974-77, 58% of the average attendance bought a copy.

DARLINGTON
Price: 20p.
Seasonal subscription: write for details to The Development Association, c/o Darlington FC Ltd, Feethams, Darlington, Teesside.
Individual copies: as above.
Club shop: situated at the ground, open match days only.

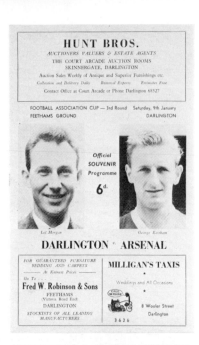
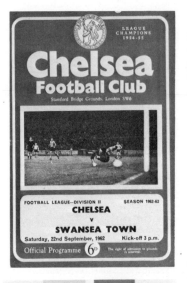

Top left: *Darlington v Arsenal, FA Cup, 1964-65.* **Top right:** *Chelsea, 1962-63.* **Above left:** *Charlton, 1974-75.* **Above:** *Palace v Hearts, 1972-73.*

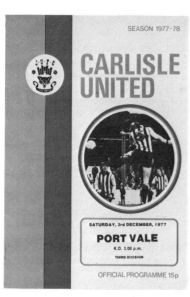

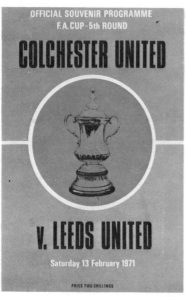

Top left: *Carlisle, 1977-78.* **Top right:** *Crewe v Spurs, FA Cup, 1959-60. Crewe held Tottenham 2-2 but lost 13-2 in the replay!* **Above left:** *Colchester v Leeds, FA Cup, 1970-71. The Division 4 side won 3-2.* **Above right:** *Bradford City v Manchester United, FL Cup, 1960-61. City won 2-1.*

DERBY COUNTY
Price: 25p (called 'The Ram').
Seasonal subscription: write for details to 'Ram' Subscription Department, Derby County FC Ltd, Baseball Ground, Derby DE3 8NB.
Individual copies: as above.
Club shop: situated by ground in Osmaston Rd, it is open on weekdays 9.00-5.30 (9.00-12.30) Wednesdays) and on match days, and stocks a wide range of programmes.
Extra information: through most of the 1970s, 'The Ram' had a newspaper format. The club switched to a magazine-style edition at the start of 1979-80, but reverted to tabloid size when it was found that the sales in outlying areas (where it was sold by newsagents) had fallen off.

DONCASTER ROVERS
Price: 20p (called 'The Rover').
Seasonal subscription: write for details to Sportscene Ltd (see Blackpool for details).
Individual copies: write to Sportscene Ltd, or to The General Office, Doncaster Rovers FC Ltd, Belle Vue, Doncaster, Yorks.
Club shop: open match days only.
Extra information: 'The Rover' has a newspaper format, and is sold locally in newsagents.

EVERTON
Price: 20p.
Seasonal subscription: write for details to The Toffee Shop, Everton FC Ltd, Goodison Park, Liverpool L4 4EL, Merseyside.
Individual copies: as above.
Club shop: as above, it is open weekdays 9.00-5.00 and on match days.
Extra information: a very informative programme, it has a full colour cover photo plus a colour centre spread.

EXETER CITY
Price: 25p.
Seasonal subscription: write for details to 'The Near Post', c/o Exeter City FC Ltd, 2 Blackboy Rd, Exeter, Devon.
Individual copies: as above.
Club shop: 'The New Post' as above; open 9.00-5.00 weekdays and on match days, they have a good selection of programmes.
Extra information: programme includes 'On Target' insert.

FULHAM
Price: 25p.
Seasonal subscription: write to Programme Subscriptions, Fulham FC Ltd, Craven Cottage, Stevenage Rd, London SW6.
Individual copies: as above.
Club shop: The 'Black & White Shop' under the Stevenage Rd stand is open on match days only and stocks a wide range of programmes.

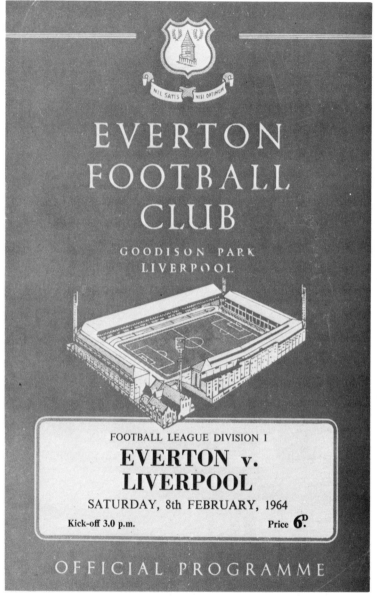

Above: *One of the world's greatest 'derbies' – Everton v Liverpool at Goodison in 1963-64. Bill Shankly's team went on to win the title, two years after gaining promotion from the Second Division – with Leyton Orient.*

Extra information: always has a good photographic and historical content. Club claim 70% of average crowd buy it.

GILLINGHAM
Price: 30p.
Seasonal subscription: write for details to The Gills Shop, 12a High St, Gillingham, Kent.
Individual copies: as above.
Club shop: The Gills Shop (as above) is open all week; also two shops at Priestfield Stadium, both open match days and selling programmes.
Extra information: programme includes 'Programme Plus' supplement.

GRIMSBY TOWN
Price: 20p (called 'The Mariner').
Seasonal subscription: write for details to The Commercial Manager, Grimsby Town FC Ltd, Blundell Park, Imperial Ave, Grimsby, South Humberside.
Individual copies: as above.
Club shop: situated in Imperial Ave, it is open weekdays 9.00-5.00 and on match days. The club always has 200 copies from previous away match on sale.

HALIFAX TOWN
Price: 20p.
Seasonal subscripton: write for details to the Commercial Manager, Halifax Town FC Ltd, 11 Horton St, Halifax, Yorks.
Individual copies: as above.
Club shop: in Horton St (as above), open weekdays 9.00-5.00.
Extra information: Halifax's programme sales reported a profit for the first time in the club's history in 1978-79 despite having their lowest-ever gates – largely due to after-sales.

HARTLEPOOL UNITED
Price: 15p.
Seasonal subscription: write to Mr. Spowart, The Club Shop, Hartlepool United FC Ltd, Victoria Ground, Hartlepool.
Individual copies: as above.
Club shop: at the ground, match days only.

HEREFORD UNITED
Price: 20p.
Seasonal subscription: write for details to The Club Shop, Hereford United FC Ltd, Edgar St, Hereford.
Individual copies: as above.
Club shop: at the ground, it is open on match days and on Wednesdays (market day) 9.00-3.00. Extensive selection of programmes.
Extra information: copies of programmes from United's Southern League days (pre-1972) are worth looking out for.

Above: *Hartlepool v Leeds, FA Cup, 1978-79. No cup shocks this time – Leeds won 6-2 – but the £17,000 Hartlepool took at the turnstiles was a record for the North-Easterners. Hartlepool have made more applications for re-election to the League than any other club, helping to make their programmes popular with collectors thinking they might lose their status.*

HULL CITY
Price: 20p.
Seasonal subscription: write for details to The General Office, Hull City FC Ltd, Boothferry Park, Hull HU4 6EH, North Humberside.
Individual copies: as above.
Club shop: One inside ground is open match days, also Tigers Shop will be opened for you if you call at the Development Office on weekdays.
Extra information: if you are in Hull, remember to visit the British Programme Club Shop.

HUDDERSFIELD TOWN
Price: 20p.
Seasonal subscription: write for details to The Secretary, Huddersfield Town FC Ltd, Leeds Rd, Huddersfield, Yorks.
Individual copies: as above.
Club shop: The Town Souvenir Shop at the ground is open on match days only. Good stock of programmes.

IPSWICH TOWN
Price: 25p.
Seasonal subscription: write for details to The Programme Department, Ipswich Town FC Ltd, Portman Rd, Ipswich, Suffolk.
Individual copies: as above.
Club shop: normally open only on match days, though if you ask at the Development Association Office, they will open it for callers.
Extra information: match day magazine has full colour cover photo, plus colour centre spread; 70% sale.

LEEDS UNITED
Price: 25p.
Seasonal subscription: write for details to The Sports & Souvenir Shop, Leeds United FC Ltd, Elland Road, Leeds LS11 0ES, Yorks.
Individual copies: write to The British Programme Club, 33 Boothferry Rd, Hull, North Humberside, who are official agents for all Leeds programmes, including back numbers.
Club shop: Sports & Souvenir Shop at the ground is open weekdays 9.30-5.30 and on match days.
Extra information: full colour cover, good photographic content.

LEICESTER CITY
Price: 30p (called 'City News')
Seasonal subscription: write to The Programme Department, Leicester City FC Ltd, Filbert St, Leicester.
Individual copies: as above.
Club shop: at ground, it is open weekdays 9.00-5.00 and on Saturdays 11.00-5.30.
Extra information: same printers and similar design to Leeds; has full colour cover.

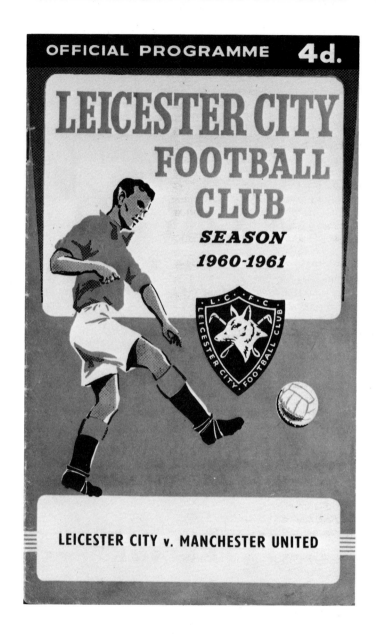

Above: *Leicester's 1960-61 edition, with Manchester United the visitors. City reached Wembley that season, only to lose 2-0 to Spurs.*

LINCOLN CITY
Price: 20p.
Seasonal subscription: write to The Secretary, Lincoln City FC Ltd, Sincil Bank, Lincoln.
Individual copies: as above.
Club shop: Red Imps Supporters Club Shop open match days.

LIVERPOOL
Price: 25p (called 'Anfield Review').
Seasonal subscription: write for details to The Secretary, Liverpool FC Ltd, Anfield Rd, Liverpool 4, Merseyside.
Individual copies: as above.
Club shop: at ground, it is open weekdays 9.30-5.30 and on match days. Liverpool aways not generally available.
Extra information: the 'Review' sells to above 60% of the club's average crowd – or about 30,000 copies per match.

LUTON TOWN
Price: 30p.
Seasonal subscription: write for details to Programme Subscriptions, Luton Town FC Ltd, Kenilworth Rd, Luton, Beds.
Individual copies: as above.
Club shop: normally open match days only, but if you ask at the Pools Office they will open it for you.
Extra information: contains 'Programme Plus' supplement.

MANCHESTER CITY
Price: 25p.
Seasonal subscription: write for details to The Souvenir Shop, Manchester City FC Ltd, Main Rd, Moss Side, Manchester M14 7WN.
Individual copies: as above.
Club shop: Souvenir Shop at ground, open weekdays 9.30-5.00 and on match days (situated next to the City Social Club).
Extra information: full colour cover, excellent historical features and photographic content.

MANCHESTER UNITED
Price: 20p (called 'United Review'.)
Seasonal subscription: write to The Programme Department, Manchester United FC Ltd, Old Trafford, Manchester M16 0RA.
Individual copies: as above.
Club shop: The Red Devils Souvenir Shop at the ground, open weekdays 9.30-4.30 and all day match days. Also two kiosks on the outside of the ground between the Stretford End and the Paddock, and in the K stand foyer at the Scoreboard End.
Extra information: United are the country's most popular club and, as such, they sometimes sell more programmes than there are spectators at the games. Sales rarely fall below 90% of the average home crowd.

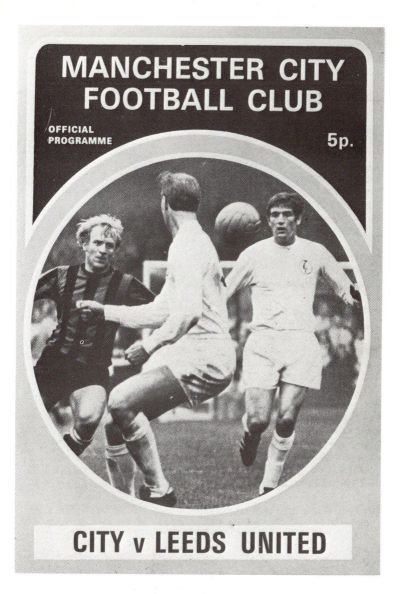

Above: *Manchester City v Leeds United on the opening day of the 1971-72 season, which ended with Leeds lifting the FA Cup for the first time in their history but failing in their last match to win the League title and the 'double'. Pictured on the cover are three England internationals – City's Francis Lee and Leeds' Jack Charlton and Norman Hunter.*

MANSFIELD TOWN
Price: 20p (called 'Stags')
Seasonal subscription: not available.
Individual copies: write to The Club Shop, Mansfield Town FC Ltd, Field Mill, Mansfield, Notts.
Club shop: as above, open weekdays 9.00-5.00 and on match days. Most Mansfield always available.

MIDDLESBROUGH
Price: 20p (called 'Boro').
Seasonal subscription: write for details to The Programme Department, Middlesbrough FC Ltd, Ayresome Park, Middlesbrough, Teesside.
Individual copies: write to the Club Shop, Middlesbrough FC Ltd, Warwick St, Middlesbrough, Teesside.
Club shop: in Warwick St, opposite main gates of the club; open weekdays 10.00-3.00 (not Wednesdays) and on match days.

MILLWALL
Price: 30p.
Seasonal subscription: write for details to The Millwall Commercial Services, 470 New Cross Rd, London SE14.
Individual copies: as above.
Club shop: three at the ground, open match days only, plus the shop in New Cross Rd (as above), which is open on weekdays 9.00-5.00.
Extra information: interesting historical feature and action photographs; also contains 'Programme Plus' supplement.

NEWCASTLE UNITED
Price: 25p.
Seasonal subscription: write for details to Inkerman Publications Ltd, Riverside Rd, Sunderland.
Individual copies: as above.
Club shop: Newcastle United Supporters Club Shop (retail outlet), 7 Prudhoe Place, Haymarket, Newcastle-on-Tyne, open weekdays 9.00-5.00; also two shops selling programmes at the ground at the East Stand and St James St, open on match days.
Extra information: programme binders are available from the Supporters Club Shop.

NEWPORT COUNTY
Price: 20p (called 'The Amber Note').
Seasonal subscription: write for details to The Programme Department, Newport County FC Ltd, Somerton Park, Newport, Gwent.
Individual copies: as above.
Club shop: a programme shop operates on match days at the ground.
Extra information: one of the outstanding editions in the lower divisions; good section of visiting team, excellent statistical information and action photos, plus historical features. Also contains 'On Target' supplement.

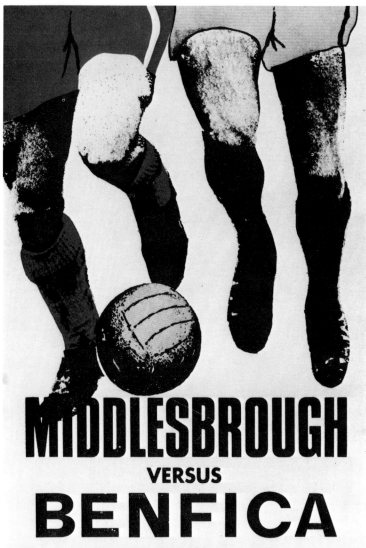

Above: *Middlesbrough v Benfica, 1971-72. Listed at number 4 for Boro in this friendly was a certain N. Stiles, and wearing 10 for the Portuguese side was Eusebio. Three years earlier they met in the European Cup final, and five years previously in England's World Cup semi-final.*

Opposite page: *One of Oxford United's first away matches as a League club – at Oldham in 1962-63.* **Above left:** *The familiar sight of Kenny Dalglish being mobbed by team-mates after yet another goal adorns the cover of Liverpool's programme for the European Super Cup match against Anderlecht of Belgium.* **Above:** *Newcastle v Leeds, 1961-62; a match that claims an important place in the Yorkshire club's success story over the next decade. Don Revie's team needed to win to be certain of avoiding the drop into Division 3. They managed just that – 3-0 and within two years were back in the First, en route for Europe.* **Left:** *Hull City v Leeds in the Second Division, 1954-55. In those days United wore gold shirts with blue sleeves and black shorts, and the 'Gentle Giant' John Charles led their attack.*

NORTHAMPTON TOWN
Price: 20p (called 'The Cobbler').
Seasonal subscription: write for details to Sportscene Ltd (see Blackpool for details).
Individual copies: as above, or from The Commercial Department, Northampton Town FC Ltd, County Ground, Northampton, Northants.
Club shop: at ground, it is open 1½ hours before the game.
Extra information: 'The Cobbler' has a newspaper format.

NORWICH CITY
Price: 30p (called 'The Canary').
Seasonal subscription: write for details to Sports Projects Ltd, 100 Wigorn Rd, Smethwick, Warley, West Midlands.
Individual copies: as above, or to The Programme Department, Norwich City FC Ltd, Carrow Rd, Norwich, Norfolk.
Club shop: Supporters Club Shop, 50 King St, Norwich (at junction of King St and Rose Lane) has limited supply of programmes.
Extra information: same printers and similar design to Bristol City, with full colour cover and colour inside.

NOTTINGHAM FOREST
Price: 20p (called 'Forest Review')
Seasonal subscription: write for details to Carrington Printers Ltd, Wilford Crescent East, Nottingham.
Individual copies: as above.
Club shop: at Clinton Rd West, Nottingham; open weekdays 9.00-5.00. Plus three shops at ground, open match days.
Extra information: traditionally an excellent programme, with strong editorial and photographic content. Particularly good issues for European games.

NOTTS COUNTY
Price: 20p.
Seasonal subscription: write for details to The Programme Department, Notts County FC Ltd, Meadow Lane, Nottingham.
Individual copies: as above.
Club shop: Souvenir Sales Shop at ground, open weekdays 9.00-5.00 and match days (at the rear of the main stand).
Extra information: County tried a newspaper format ('The Magpie') for a while, but have now reverted to a more traditional style.

OLDHAM ATHLETIC
Price: 20p.
Seasonal subscription: write to The Programme Department, Oldham Athletic FC Ltd, Boundary Park, Oldham, Lancs.
Individual copies: as above.
Club shop: The Latics Shop at ground is open weekdays 9.00-5.00 and on match days.

Above: *Norwich City's first-ever match in the First Division, against Everton at Carrow Road on the opening day of 1972-73. The Canaries' stay in the top flight lasted only two seasons, but they needed only one season back in the Second to gain promotion again in 1974-75.*

Extra information: Oldham poineered the newspaper-style now favoured by several clubs with their 'Boundary Bulletin' in the 1960s, although they soon changed back and have been publishing a more traditional programme for several years now.

ORIENT
Price: 25p.
Seasonal subcription: not available.
Individual copies: write for details to The Commercial Centre, Orient FC Ltd, 369 High Rd, London E10.
Club shop: as above, open weekdays; also by main entrance at the grounds in Brisbane Rd, match days only.
Extra information: the club were known as Leyton Orient from 1946-67, and programmes bearing that name are well worth keeping an eye out for.

OXFORD UNITED
Price: 25p.
Seasonal subscription: write for details to The Programme Department, Oxford United FC Ltd, Manor Ground, Beech Rd, Oxford.
Individual copies: as above.
Club shop: on the ground, open on match days only, although they will open if you ask at the club on weekdays.
Extra information: Until 1960 the club were known as Headington United, and they were members of the Southern League until 1962. Programmes from this era are particularly valuable.

PETERBOROUGH UNITED
Price: 20p.
Seasonal subscription: not available.
Individual copies: write to The Commercial Department, Peterborough United FC Ltd, London Rd, Peterborough PE2 8AL.
Club shop: The Posh Shop at the ground is open on match days only.
Extra information: another highly distinctive edition from the lower divisions. Also watch for the club's Midland League programmes prior to their election to the Fourth in 1960.

PLYMOUTH ARGYLE
Price: 25p.
Seasonal subscription: write for details to The Programme Manager, The Pilgrim Shop, Plymouth Argyle FC Ltd, Home Park, Plymouth, Devon.
Individual copies: as above.
Club shops: as above, open weekdays 9.00-5.00 and on match days.

PORTSMOUTH
Price: 20p.
Seasonal subscription: write for details to The Pompey Shop, Portsmouth FC Ltd, Fratton Park, Portsmouth, Hants.
Individual copies: as above.

Above: *'Mr Posh' looks happy enough as Peterborough face the Italian Olympic XI at the start of 1967-68. But at the end of the season United were demoted to Division 4 for financial irregularities.*

Club shop: as above, it is situated at 42 Frogmore Rd, open weekdays 9.30-5.00 and until 10.00pm after evening matches.

PORT VALE
Price: 20p.
Seasonal subscription: not available.
Individual copies: write to The General Office, Port Vale FC Ltd, Vale Park, Hamil Rd, Burslem, Stoke-on-Trent ST6 1AW.
Club shop: sells many souvenirs, but no programmes.
Extra information: copies from the club's previous ground at Bryan Street, Hanley are particularly valuable.

PRESTON NORTH END
Price: 20p (called 'The North Ender').
Seasonal subscription: write for details to The Commercial Manager, Preston North End FC Ltd, Deepdale, Preston, Lancs or to Sportscene Ltd (see Blackpool for details).
Individual copies: write to the Commercial Manager, as above.
Club shop: The Lilywhites Souvenir Shop, at ground, is open on match days only.
Extra information: newspaper-style edition.

QUEEN'S PARK RANGERS
Price: 25p.
Seasonal subscription: write for details to The General Office, QPR FC Ltd, South Africa Rd, London W12.
Individual copies: as above.
Club shop: Supporters Club Shop at ground, open weekdays 9.00-5.00, and on match days.
Extra information: Rangers sell a programme to 8 out of every 10 of their average crowd; programme has particularly fine colour photos and contains no advertisements.

READING
Price: 20p.
Seasonal subscription: write for details to The Supporters Club Shop, Reading FC Ltd, Elm Park, Reading, Berkshire.
Individual copies: as above.
Club shop: two shops at ground, in Norfolk Rd and on West Terrace, on match days only.

ROCHDALE
Price: 20p (called 'The Dale').
Seasonal subscription: write to Sportscene Ltd (see Blackpool for details).
Individual copies: write to Programme Department, Rochdale FC Ltd, Spotland, Rochdale, Lancs.
Club shop: Supporters Club booth on match days.
Extra information: newspaper format.

Above: *QPR's first-ever match in the First Division, at home to Leicester on the first day of 1968-69. Rangers had come from the Third to the First in successive seasons but finished bottom at the end of this season.*

ROTHERHAM UNITED
Price: 20p (called 'The Miller').
Seasonal subscription: write for details to Rotherham United Promotions, Millmoor, Rotherham, Yorks or to Sportscene Ltd (see Blackpool for details).
Individual copies: as above.
Extra information: newspaper format.

SCUNTHORPE UNITED
Price: 15p.
Seasonal subscription: not available.
Individual copies: write to The General Office, Scunthorpe United FC Ltd, Old Show Ground, Scunthorpe, Lincs.
Club shop: adjacent to the Promotions Office at the ground, it is open on match days only.

SHEFFIELD UNITED
Price: 25p.
Seasonal subscription: write for details to The Lane Souvenir Shop, Sheffield United FC Ltd, John St, Sheffield S2 4SU.
Individual copies: as above.
Club shop: as above, open weekday lunchtimes 12.00-2.00 and from 9.30 am on match days.
Extra information: United produce an attractive programme, although they are among many clubs who report a drop in sales at night matches.

SHEFFIELD WEDNESDAY
Price: 25p (called 'The Owl')
Seasonal subscription: write for details to The Commercial Department, Sheffield Wednesday FC Ltd, Hillsborough, Sheffield S6 1SW.
Individual copies: as above.
Club shop: the Owls Shop at ground, open weekdays 10.00-4.00 (not Thursday) and on match days.
Extra information: like their neighbours, Wednesday have continued to produce an excellent magazine despite falling into the lower divisions.

SHREWSBURY TOWN
Price: 20p (called 'Town Times')
Seasonal subscription: write for details to The Promotions Office, Shrewsbury Town FC Ltd, Gay Meadow, Shrewsbury, Salop.
Individual copies: as above.
Club shop: at ground, open match days only.
Extra information: newspaper format.

SOUTHEND UNITED
Price: 30p.
Seasonal subscription: not available.
Individual copies: write to The Club Shop, Southend United FC Ltd, 374

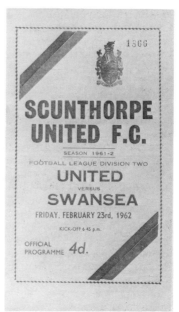

Above left: *Sheffield United v Notts County, a Second Division match from 1956-57. In those days the Blades shared Bramall Lane with Yorkshire County Cricket Club – hence the large area on one side of the pitch in the drawing on the programme cover.* **Above:** *Scunthorpe United v Swansea Town, also a Second Division fixture, from 1961-62. Scunthorpe have been in the Fourth since 1968 apart from one season.* **Left:** *Shrewsbury Town v Port Vale, Division 3, 1972-73.*

Victoria Ave, Southend, Essex.
Club shop: as above, at ground; open weekdays 9.00-5.00 and on match days.
Extra information: contains 'Programme Plus' supplement.

SOUTHAMPTON
Price: 25p.
Seasonal subscription: write for details to The Club Shop, Southampton FC Ltd, The Dell, Milton Rd, Southampton, Hants.
Individual copies: as above.
Club shop: at ground, open weekdays 9.00-5.00 and on match days: the club runs two other shops, in the city centre and on the Isle of Wight, but these do not sell programmes.
Extra information: above average production.

STOCKPORT COUNTY
Price: 20p.
Seasonal subscription: not available.
Individual copies: write to The General Office, Stockport County FC Ltd, Edgely Park Stockport, Cheshire.
Club shop: no.

STOKE CITY
Price: 30p.
Seasonal subscription: write for details to The General Office, Stoke City FC Ltd, Victoria Ground, Stoke-on-Trent, Staffs.
Individual copies: as above.
Club shop: Bourne Sports in Church St, Stoke is the club shop, but it does not stock programmes.
Extra information: contains 'Programme Plus' supplement.

SUNDERLAND
Price: 25p (called 'Roker Review').
Seasonal subscription: write for details to Inkerman Publications Ltd, Riverside Rd, Sunderland.
Individual copies: as above.
Club shop: at ground, Roker Park, open weekdays 9.00-5.00 and on match days.

SWANSEA CITY
Price: 25p.
Seasonal subscription: write for details to The Commercial Department, Swansea City FC Ltd, 33 William St, Swansea.
Individual copies: as above.
Club shop: as above, in William St; open weekdays 9.00-5.00 and on match days.
Extra information: the club was known as Swansea Town until 1970 – watch for issues bearing that name.

Above: *A South Coast 'derby' between Southampton and Portsmouth in the Second Division, 1963-64. Saints' history includes a spell in the Third Division, whereas Pompey have two League titles to their name. Yet as the 1980s began, the clubs were four divisions apart.*

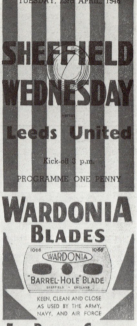
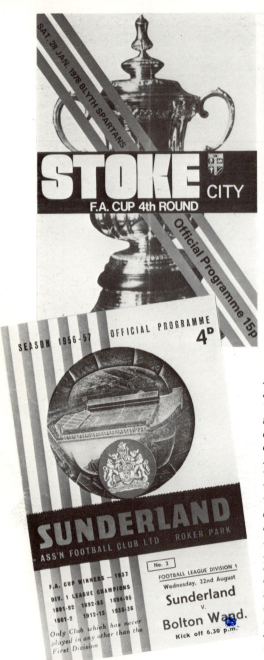

Above left: *Stoke v Blyth Spartans, FA Cup, 1977-78. This game provided one of the Cup's finest giant-killing acts, the Northern League amateurs winning 3-2.*
Above: *Sheffield Wednesday v Leeds, played in the last wartime season, 1945-46, when matches were played on a regional basis.* **Left:** *Sunderland v Bolton, a First Division fixture from 1956-57. In the bottom left-hand corner is the proud claim: 'only club which has never played in any other than the First Division.' By the end of the following season, 1957-58, Sunderland had been relegated.*

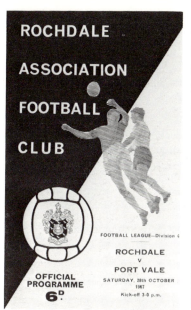
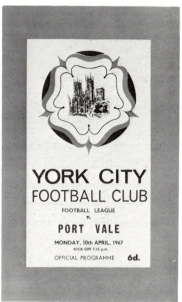

Above left: *Rochdale v Port Vale, 1967-68.* **Above:** *York City's 1966-67 edition, with Port Vale again the visitors.* **Left:** *'Go Go Go County' was one of Stockport County's slogans for 1966-67, when they won the Fourth Divison title. Another was 'Friday night is County night', a reference to their tendency to avoid fixture clashes with the Manchester clubs by playing on Friday evenings. The crowds were sizeable – there were over 10,000 at this game with Bradford City.*

SWINDON TOWN
Price: 20p.
Seasonal subscription: write for details to The Secretary, Swindon FC Ltd, County Ground, Swindon, Wiltshire.
Individual copies: as above.
Club shop: The Souvenir Shop at ground; open on match days only.

TORQUAY UNITED
Price: 25p.
Seasonal subscription: write for details to Promotions Department, Torquay United FC Ltd, Plainmoor, Torquay, Devon.
Individual copies: as above.
Club shop: The Gulls Shop, at ground; match days only, but they will open it specially for you on weekdays if you call.
Extra information: full colour cover, superb section on visiting club plus two pages of action – with Newport and Bournemouth, probably the best in the Fourth in 1979-80. Also contains 'On Target' supplement.

TOTTENHAM HOTSPUR
Price: 25p.
Seasonal subscription: write for details to The Spurs Shop, 1/3 Park Lane, London N17.
Individual copies: as above.
Club shop: as above, it is situated at the junction of High Rd and Park Lane; open weekdays 9.00-5.00 (Thursdays 9.00-1.00) and on match days. The Spurs Supporters Club also has a programme booth outside its premises at 744 High Rd, by main entrance.
Extra information: very few adverts, news of all Spurs' teams, historical feature called 'Scrapbook', plus two pages of colour action photos and full colour cover. When Spurs won the 'double' in 1960-61, their programme was a four-pager – no adverts, but no photos.

TRANMERE ROVERS
Price: 20p (called 'the Prenton').
Seasonal subscription: from Sportscene Ltd (see Blackpool for details).
Individual copies: write to Tranmere Rovers Supporters Association, Prenton Park, Birkenhead, Merseyside.
Club shop: The Supporters Shop, at ground; open match days only.
Extra information: another newspaper-programme. Tranmere is one of the clubs whose small crowds mean their survival is always threatened; like Crewe and Rochdale, well worth collecting.

WALSALL
Price: 20p (called 'The Saddler').
Seasonal subscription: from Sportscene Ltd (see Blackpool for details).
Individual copies: as above.
Club shop: 'The Saddlers Shop', at ground; open match days only.
Extra information: newspaper format.

Above: *The night European football came to Birkenhead: Tranmere Rovers entertain Victoria Berlin in a friendly in 1959-60. The German club were Prenton Park's first-ever visitors from outside the British Isles.*

WATFORD
Price: 25p.
Seasonal subscription: write for details to Watford FC Ltd, Vicarage Rd, Watford, Herts.
Individual copies: as above.
Club shop: at ground; open all week 9.00-5.00, and on match days.
Extra information: full colour cover.

WEST BROMWICH ALBION
Price: 30p (called 'Albion News').
Seasonal subscription: write for details to The Commercial Manager, West Bromwich Albion Ltd, Halfords Lane, West Bromwich, Staffs.
Individual copies: as above.
Club shop: c/o Pools Office, at ground; open weekdays 9.00-5.00, and on match days.
Extra information: traditionally one of the League's best, it was voted number 1 in the Commercial Managers' Association poll in 1979; fine action pix, superb historical features.

WEST HAM UNITED
Price: 25p (called 'The Hammer').
Seasonal subscription: write for details to Helliar & Son, 237 Barking Rd, London E13 8EQ.
Individual copies: as above.
Club shop: 'Hammers Shop', at ground; open weekdays 10.00-4.00 (not Tuesdays) and on match days.
Extra information: still pocket-sized issue with few adverts and plenty of detailed statistical information.

WIGAN ATHLETIC
Price: 20p.
Seasonal subscription: write for details to The Soccer Shop, Wigan Athletic FC Ltd, Springfield Park, Wigan, Lancs.
Individual copies: as above.
Club shop: as above, open all week and on match days.
Extra information: Wigan programmes from their non-League days are becoming more valuable all the time, and the Club Shop still has stocks as well as some from their first League season, 1978-79.

WIMBLEDON
Price: 25p.
Seasonal subscription: write for details to The Secretary, Wimbledon FC Ltd, Plough Lane, London SW19.
Individual copies: as above.
Club shop: 'The Dons Shop' at ground (adjacent to 'The Sportsman' pub); open weekdays 9.00-5.00 and on match days.
Extra information: few adverts, high photo content; Wimbledon's programme has improved enormously since they joined the League.

Above: 'Albion News', the colourful West Bromwich Albion programme. On the cover of this 1977-78 issue for a League match against Leeds, Derek Statham was the featured player, and inside the reader is informed that Statham is known to his team-mates as 'Wolverhampton'!
Right: West Ham's 'Hammer', an edition from the London 'derby' with Chelsea in 1972-73.

Wimbledon Football Club

FOUNDED 1889

Members of
The Football Association
London Football Association
Surrey Football Association
The Amateur Football Alliance
and The Isthmian League

Ground: Plough Lane,
Wimbledon, S.W.19
Tel.: WIMbledon 1993

Hon. Secretary:
B. C. CORKE,
28 Boltons Close, Pyrford, Surrey

Hon. Press Secretary:
ALEC FUCE,
50 Galveston Road, S.W.15
Tel.: VANdyke 4771

PRESIDENT: SIR CYRIL BLACK, J.P., D.L., M.P.

ISTHMIAN LEAGUE — SENIOR SECTION

SATURDAY, 19th NOVEMBER, 1960

WIMBLEDON

v

ST. ALBANS CITY

KICK OFF 3.00 P.M.

---

* Repairs and Maintenance
* Petrol and Oils
* Accessories and Tyres
* Cars for Weddings, etc.

PARK MOTOR WORKS

LIB. 2606   290 HAYDONS ROAD

Official Programme   *Season 1960/61*   Price 3d.

Above: *Wimbledon v St Albans – an Isthmian League programme from 1960-61. The same season Sheffield Wednesday were runners-up to Spurs' double side. By 1979-80 they were meeting in the Third Divison.*

Top: *A year after the appearance of Coventry's 'Sky Blue', the first edition of Wolves' match-day magazine 'Molinews' went on sale at the match against QPR on the opening day of 1968-69.* **Centre:** *Walsall's 'modern art' cover design for the 1972-73 season.* **Above:** *Watford's programme for 1972-73 made good use of the club's nickname – 'The Hornets'.*

WOLVERHAMPTON WANDERERS
Price: 25p.
Seasonal Subscription: write for details to The Commercial Department, Wolverhampton Wanderers FC Ltd, Molineux, Wolverhampton WV1 4QR, West Midlands.
Individual copies: as above.
Club shop: 'The Lair', at ground; open match days only.

WREXHAM
Price: 20p.
Seasonal subscription: write for details to 'The Centre Spot', Wrexham FC Ltd, Mold Rd, Wrexham, N. Wales.
Individual copies: as above.
Club shop: 'The Centre Spot' at ground, open weekdays 10.00-2.00 (not Wednesdays) and on match days.

YORK CITY
Price: 10p.
Seasonal subscription: write for details to The Secretary, York City FC Ltd, Bootham Crescent, York.
Individual copies: as above.
Club shop: at ground, on match days only; extensive selection of non-League and Scottish programmes available.
Extra information: York will arrange a subscription which includes programmes from all their away matches.

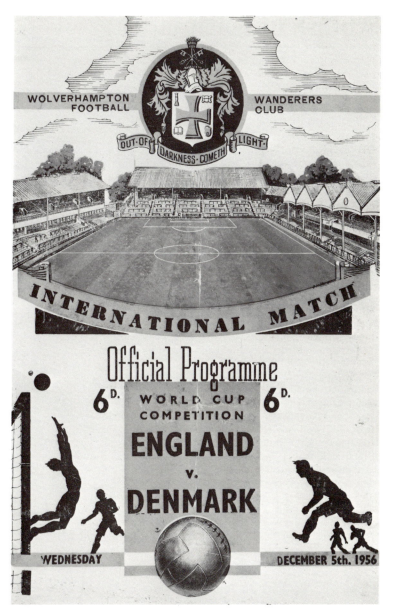

Above: *Wolves staged England's World Cup qualifying match against Denmark in 1956. England won 5-2, with a hat-trick by Tommy Taylor and two from Duncan Edwards. Both were victims of the 1958 Munich disaster.*

Scottish League Clubs

Write direct to the clubs at the following addresses, always remembering to enclose a stamped addressed envelope.

Aberdeen: Pittodrie Stadium, Aberdeen.
Airdrieonians: Broomfield Park, Airdrie, Lanarkshire.
Albion Rovers: Cliftonhill Park, Coatbridge, Lanarkshire.
Alloa Athletic: Recreation Ground, Alloa, Clackmannanshire.
Arbroath: Gayfield Park, Arbroath, Angus.
Ayr United: Somerset Park, Ayr, Ayrshire.
Berwick Rangers: Shielfield Park, Berwick-on-Tweed, Northumberland.
Brechin City: Glebe Park, Brechin, Angus.
Celtic: Celtic Park, Parkhead, Glasgow.
Clyde: Shawfield Stadium, Glasgow.
Clydebank: Kilbowie Park, Clydebank, Renfrewshire.
Cowdenbeath: Central Park, Cowdenbeath, Fife.
Dumbarton: Boghead Park, Dumbarton, Dumbartonshire.
Dundee: Dens Park, Dundee, Tayside.
Dundee United: Tannadice Park, Dundee, Tayside.
Dunfermline Athletic: East End Park, Dunfermline, Fife.
East Fife: Bayview Park, Methil, Fife.
East Stirlingshire: Firs Park, Falkirk, Stirlingshire.
Falkirk: Brockville Park, Falkirk, Stirlingshire.
Forfar Athletic: Station Park, Forfar, Angus.
Hamilton Academicals: Douglas Park, Hamilton, Lanarkshire.
Heart of Midlothian: Tynecastle Park, Gorgie Rd, Edinburgh.
Hibernian: Easter Road Park, Edinburgh.
Kilmarnock: Rugby Park, Kilmarnock, Ayrshire.
Meadowbank Thistle: Meadowbank Stadium, Edinburgh.
Montrose: Links Park, Montrose, Angus.
Morton: Cappielow Park, Greenock, Renfrewshire.
Motherwell: Fir Park, Motherwell, Lanarkshire.
Partick Thistle: Firhill Park, Glasgow NW.
Queen of the South: Palmerston Park, Dumfries, Dumfrieshire.
Queen's Park: Hampden Park, Glasgow.
Raith Rovers: Starks Park, Kirkaldy, Fife.
Rangers: Ibrox Stadium, Glasgow.
St Johnstone: Muirton Park, Perth, Perthshire.
St Mirren: Love Street, Paisley, Renfrewshire.
Stenhousemuir: Ochilview Park, Stenhousemuir.
Stirling Albion: Annfield Park, Stirling, Stirlingshire.
Stranraer: Stair Park, Stranraer, Wigtownshire.

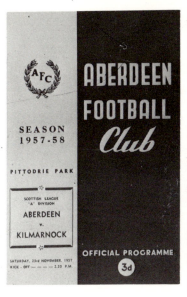

Top left: *Aberdeen, 1957-58.* **Top right:** *Hibernian v Newcastle, 1955-56, when both clubs were major powers in British football.* **Above left:** *East Fife, 1964-65.* **Above right:** *Another Scottish v English 'friendly' – Glasgow Rangers v Tottenham Hotspur, 1971-72.*

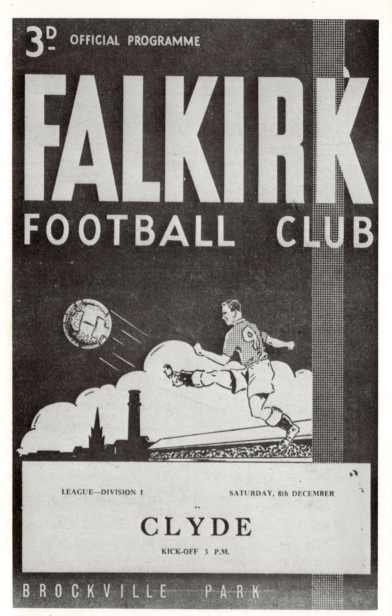

Above: *Falkirk v Clyde, 1962-63. This Scottish First Division match produced an outstanding individual performance by Falkirk striker Hugh Maxwell, who scored seven goals.*

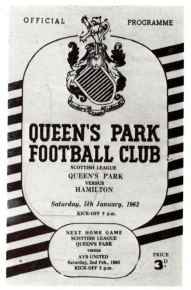
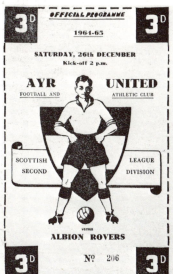

Top left: *Morton v Chelsea, a floodlit 'friendly' from 1962-63.* **Top right:** *Queen's Park, 1962-63; the famous Glasgow club remain amateur to this day.* **Above left:** *Ayr United, 1964-65.* **Above:** *Celtic, 1971-72; the shamrock on the cover indicates the club's Irish Catholic origins.*

Programme Shops and Clubs

The British Programme Club Shop: 33 Boothferry Rd, Hull, North Humberside. Open Mon-Fri 7.00am-1.00 and Sats.
The Football Fan: 44 Yorkshire St, Burnley, Lancs. Open Mon-Sat 10.00am-5.00.
The Programme Cabin: 286 Leeds Rd, Hawden Clough, Birstall, West Yorks.
Spot Programme Shop: 2 Maes Las, Main Rd, Llantwit Fardre, Pontypridd, South Wales.
Manchester Programme & Souvenir Centre: 784 Wilmslow Rd, Didsbury, Manchester 20.
The Footballer Shop: 1 Longshaw St, Bolton Rd, Blackburn, Lancs. Open six days a week.
The British Programme Club: 33 Boothferry Rd, Hull, North Humberside.
The Thameside Programme Club: 8 Stapleford Gardens, Romford RM5 2JT, Essex.
The Wirral Programme Club: 3 Tansley Close, West Kirby, Merseyside L48 9XH.
The Scottish Programme Club: 34 Coldstream Drive, Rutherglen, Glasgow G73 3LH.